AFRO

VEGAN

Afro Vegan
First Edition

First published in the United Kingdom in 2021 by Hoxton Mini Press.
Copyright © Hoxton Mini Press 2021
All rights reserved

Photography and text © Zoe Alakija 2021*
Edited by Harry Adès
Design by Daniele Roa
Art direction by Zoe Alakija
Recipe testing and styling advice by Emily Kydd
Production by Anna De Pascale
Image retouching support by Becca Jones
Copy editing by Florence Filose

*Except for the images on p.10–11 © Tolu Adekuoroye 2017

The right of Zoe Alakija to be identified as the creator of this Work has been
asserted under the Copyright, Designs and Patents Act 1988.

With thanks to our Kickstarter backers who invested in our future:
Andrew, Laura and Raphael Beaumont, Anonymous, David Rix,
Don McConnell, Duncan, Liss and Theo, Fiona and Gordon (Bow),
Gareth Tennant, Gary, Graham McClelland, Herlinde, Jenifer Roberts,
Jennifer Barnaby, Joe Skade, Jonathan Crown, Jonathan J. N. Taylor,
Matt Jackson, Melissa O'Shaughnessy, Nigel S, Rob Phillips,
Rory Cooper, Simon Robinson and Steev A. Toth.

ISBN: 978-1-910566-90-9

A CIP catalogue record for this book is available from the British Library

Printed and bound by OZGraf, Poland

Hoxton Mini Press is an environmentally conscious publisher, committed to offsetting
our carbon footprint. The offset for this book was purchased from Stand For Trees.

For every book you buy from our website, we plant a tree:
www.hoxtonminipress.com

ZOE ALAKIJA

AFRO VEGAN

Family recipes from
a British-Nigerian kitchen

Edited by Harry Adès

HOXTON MINI PRESS

CONTENTS

SOUPS, STEWS & SWALLOWS

MAINS

SIDES & SNACKS

DIPS & SAUCES

SWEET TREATS

DRINKS

Oun tá
ó jẹ ṣe
pàtàkì ju
oun tá
ó ṣe

What we want to eat is more important
than what we want to do

Sundays
in Ibadan

I close my eyes and I'm back home. The West African sun beats down, and the air is thick with birdsong and barbecue smoke. Toasted cumin and devil pepper wafts through the air, as Dad is put to work, charring lunch on the grill. It's Sunday in Ibadan, the lively city in Nigeria where I grew up.

The clink of cutlery and crockery folds into the harmonies of the neighbourhood children, chanting Sunday school anthems. We crowd around the frying plantain, listening to the oil sizzle, begging for a crunchy morsel before lunch.

In the afternoon, we go to Maggie's salon to have our braids done. Every aunty entering is bemused by the òyìnbó (European) getting tight cornrows; my mother is as British as they come, and my father British-Nigerian, so yes, I do look quite white. Afterwards, at Mokola Market, we buy crested chameleons to free in our garden, and watch as they disappear into the thick of heliconia and hibiscus.

We watch Dad play polo, and at sunset we have dinner with the players: spice-rubbed suya kebabs (p.84) and dodo (p.99), and a fizzy malt drink, Maltina. Chilli sauce spatters across our clothes, as we drench our plates.

As night draws in, my grandfather Ogie's car breaks the stillness; he has brought ice cream from the factory down the road. We point to where we still have room in our stomachs, even after a day of gorging on our favourite foods with our favourite people.

This book is an ode to those Sundays. I dedicate it to the memory of my dad.

Me (in the spotty dress), my twin brother
Carl (back left) and our friends Gbinda (front left) and
Ngila (right), with my dad, Adeyemo, in 1998.

From top left in clockwise order:
A street vendor in Ibadan selling wara,
a popular cheese-like snack that can be
made from cow's milk or soya;
a colourful photo of Ibadan, also known
as 'the brown roof city' for obvious
reasons; washing peppers and tomatoes
at a local market; in Nigeria, importing
new furniture has been restricted to
support sales of locally made cane
furnishings, like these woven floor mats.

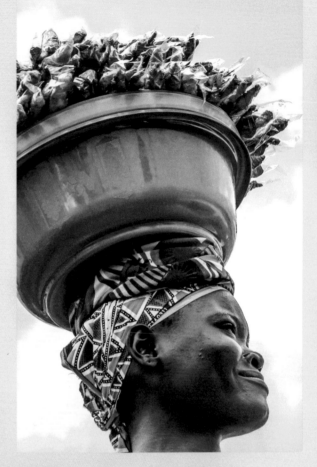

This page, from top left in clockwise order: Fishermen mending nets on Agaja Beach, just outside of Lagos – seafood is a commonly used ingredient in Nigerian food, even seemingly vegetarian dishes are often seasoned with crayfish, which can make finding vegan meals tricky; my dad, Grandma Audri, Aunty Keffi and Aunty Teju in the 80s; my sister Rita as a baby in 1999, with a friend of our family.

This page, from top in clockwise order: My youngest sister Alyx with our giant African tortoise, Toytoys, at our family home in Ibadan in 2000; a cassava peeler working on my brother Carl's farm in Oyo state; me (left) and Cousin Saphie on Agaja Beach in 1996.

This page, from top in clockwise order:
My mom (Polly), Dad and Grandma
Audri canoeing through the Agaja
lagoon in 1994; my grandfather's
lovely cook Kwaku, who is famous for
his amazing smile and unbelievably
spicy chilli sauce (p.124); Aunty Keffi
(whose recipe for coconut chips is
in this book, p.112) on Agaja Beach
in the 70s.

This page, from top left in clockwise order: My dad eating a fresh coconut in the early 2000s; cassava crops; a Ghanaian street vendor selling cocoa pods, pure honey and coconuts in Lagos.

Me at home in London, 2021.

Finding My Home
Through Food

The Golden Dragon was one of the few reputable restaurants near my childhood home in Nigeria, and we were almost permanent fixtures. When it temporarily shut down, we spent our family days cooking up a storm in our kitchen, which we playfully called The Silver Dragon. The food wasn't nearly as good, but every new creation was a joy of experimentation and shared endeavour. Above all, I realised that food brings people together like nothing else. My love of cooking was born.

The first cake I baked, a loudly eccentric five-layer confection for my youngest sister's seventh birthday, was a wobbly, rainbow of a mess – and a complete eyesore. Since then, my tastes have thankfully evolved, drawing on my joint British and Nigerian upbringing. My father was proudly Yorùbá, one of the largest and most ancient cultures in Nigeria. He and my mother met at school in England when they were both 16, and moved to Ibadan together to start our family shortly after.

Having inherited both my mother and father's cultures, developing my own sense of cultural belonging has been troublesome. Living between London, where I'm based now, and Ibadan, which are about as different as any two places could be, I have at times felt disconnected from both – as if they were moulds that I couldn't hope to crack.

But I have felt firmly within each world, too. Eventually, I learnt the beautiful side of my predicament: versatility. This book is born of that versatility, an integration of my mixed heritage, of merged cultures and diverse influences, that shapes and channels the flavours, ingredients and cookery of these dishes. It's the story of how I found home through food.

Zoe

Afro Vegan?

Yes, *Afro Vegan*. Yes, an utter contradiction. Here in your hands is a vegan recipe book that draws its breath from the explosive colours, contrasts, cultures and flavours of West Africa – or more specifically, western Nigeria.

How? It's a region where dishes heavily feature game, meat, eggs and dairy. This was the food of my childhood, but as an adult my concerns about animal cruelty and the environment introduced me to the world of veganism. Now, when I'm at home in Nigeria as a vegan, it's almost comical trying to find something that's good and vegan to eat. Despite this, the region's cuisine is actually remarkably easily adapted to veganism. The hard work of the cookery, where the magic is really happening, is never solely borne by animal-derived products.

Sauces, bases and stews bubble away over hours; tomatoes, Scotch bonnets and legumes mingle their flavours with spices familiar and exotic – chilli, cumin, ginger, irú, ehuru. Huge trenchers of spiced rice, festooned with vegetables or toasted coconut, enlivened by crispy fried onion and the zing of lime juice and chilli sauce, are the centrepieces of our everyday dining table. Ground cassava, pounded yam and oatmeal serve as the basis for a kind of edible cutlery as 'swallows', carb-rich balls of energy used to mop up soups and stews. And a weakness for deep-fried food, such as doughy puff-puff (p.141) adorning heaving platters of 'small chops', means an obligatory array of delicacies at any Nigerian party. With all this going on, you could imagine that the meat component, although ubiquitous, is not so much the star of the kitchen, but almost an afterthought to the main event.

To flip the coin, you might also ask how veganism can sit comfortably within the boisterous colour of West African cooking. Vegans can truly get a terrible rep, from settling for drab and cardboardy substitutes, to obsessions with hard-to-find foods with a mighty price tag. It doesn't have to be like that. Vegans can enjoy colour, exuberance, spice, flavour and natural ingredients as much as anyone else – and will certainly flourish in the warm glow and endless comfort of Nigerian food. In fact, there's a growing community of 'Afro vegans' sharing recipes online in some excellent blogs. And easy, accessible ingredients can be just as delicious as the unusual items you might have to track down in a specialist supermarket. Plantain, hibiscus, pomegranate, okra, mango, honey beans, peanuts, chickpeas, beetroot: simple or special, there's always excitement and colour and taste here – which will appeal to anyone interested in food, vegan or not.

To say there's a great diversity of styles within West African cuisine doesn't really scratch the surface. You'll find big differences across a single Nigerian state alone. The cooking typical of the south west, around Ibadan where I grew up, is the bedrock of the combinations and ingredients of this book, often underpinned by earthy red palm oil that's sustainably produced and used so much in the area. But, like the peoples of the region at large, I have been a magpie, taking my favourites from all around.

In the north of the country, for instance, where millet, sorghum and peanut are commonly grown, you'll find kebabs sold in the streets smothered in suya spice that mixes roasted peanuts, cayenne and ground ginger to devastating effect. The combination is just as good on vegetables (p.84), coconut chips (p.112), pulses (p.121) and much else. The recipes in this book are playfully inauthentic, born of my own experience and individual taste. It's fair to say, however, that the way the majority of the ingredients in these dishes interact with each other – even such straightforward ones as tomatoes, peppers and onions when stewed together with chilli to form a thick base – is singularly, distinctively and universally Nigerian.

Nigeria has its own external influences, too. There is a small but well-established Lebanese-Nigerian community tucked away in the south west. It's to them I owe the fonio tabbouleh (p.53) and chickpea shawarma (p.58) recipes. Few realise that there's also a deep underlying connection between Nigeria and Brazil, not least in my own family, which once had the given Brazilian name Assumpção before my ancestors chose Alakija on return to our homeland. They numbered among the many Yorùbá returnees, also known as Amaros or Agudás, from Brazilian plantations. The link between the two countries is no better expressed than in àkàrà, a fried bean fritter (p.94), introduced to Brazil by Nigerians, which remains an important dish in Yorùbá cultures on both sides of the Atlantic.

My cooking is further shaped by my time in London. I first came to England for school at age 16, stayed for university and have lived in London ever since; so now I also see myself as a Londoner, and as a Brit. Everything I have grown up with passes through this filter too, one that I think of as 'ultra-modern' in comparison with the ancient traditional cooking of West Africa – but, really, they are as ancient and modern as each other in their own ways. The result is a diversity of dishes that takes the best of all worlds, a kaleidoscope of colours and flavours that will surprise and delight, while staying somehow familiar no matter where you're standing. In the end, though, food has a talent for talking for itself; so all there is to do now is cook, eat, share and enjoy!

Afro-Vegan Ingredients

As any cook will tell you, every ingredient is important in its own way for any given recipe. But here I've picked out 12 that I think are among the key characters in the Nigerian vegan kitchen and great starting points for further exploration. (And I'm not including staples like pepper, tomato, onion and rice, which many Nigerians would argue are the most important of all!) Some of these additions are easier to find than others; here's hoping that West African cuisine soon takes the mainstream market by storm, but until we see oloyin beans and hibiscus in supermarket aisles, I'd urge you to explore your local Afro-Caribbean markets and speciality stores. Failing that, you can find a wide range of ingredients via the internet, particularly through the usual suspects, Google, Amazon and eBay, and I've suggested a few easy alternatives in the recipes.

Nigerian honey bean (oloyin) [1]

Thanks to its distinctive sweetness, this is the go-to bean to use for àkàrà (p.94) or miyan wake (p.35), preferably whole but you can also find it as a flour. Unfortunately, these beans can be tricky to track down outside of Nigeria, but you can definitely get away with using black-eyed beans instead.

Cashew [2]

Cashew trees grow everywhere in Nigeria in the wild, in fact my childhood home was on a cashew 'farm' in Oyo state – more a stretch of wilderness with the odd field of crops among natural ponds.

Coconut [3]

Coconut palms dot the skyline all over Nigeria, and coconuts are used in many forms – desiccated, raw, as flour, milk, cream, water or oil – in savouries, sweets and snacks.

Garri [4]

A coarse flour with an undeniably sour taste, made by grating, mashing, pressing, fermenting and frying or toasting cassava. It's used for èbà (p.29), coating crunchy kokoro (p.96), or stirred into ice-cold water with sugar and peanuts to eat as a cereal (which is called soakis).

Groundnut [5]

Groundnut is the word Nigerians use for peanut. Nigeria grows more groundnuts than any other country in Africa. No wonder we use them so much in our cooking – for sauces, oil and stews (p.36) or ground up to coat suya kebabs (p.84) – or just to nibble on, dry roasted (p.116).

Hibiscus [6]

Of the many types of hibiscus growing across West Africa, it's the blood-red flowers of *Hibiscus sabdariffa* that are prized for their dry, fruity flavour, particularly for zobo punch (p.166).

Yam [7]

Yam, or puna yam in Nigeria, is a root vegetable prevalent across West Africa. They're much starchier but less sweet than sweet potatoes (which Americans confusingly also call yams), and have high cultural value, celebrated annually in the New Yam Festival at the end of the rainy season. Yam is often roughly chopped and stirred into savoury stews (p.46); boiled and spiced with paprika (isu); sliced, deep-fried and served as a side; or pounded for swallows (p.29).

Scotch bonnet [8]

These fiery chilli peppers (ata rodo) have a distinctively sweet tomato-like flavour and are recognisable by their short, round shape, and rainbow colours: yellow, red, green and orange. They're nearly ubiquitous in Nigerian cuisine. However, if you're not able to track them down outside of West Africa, you can use habanero chillies instead. I would recommend wearing gloves when preparing Scotch bonnets, and definitely avoiding touching your eyes or mouth – they're seriously hot. If you're not a fan of too much heat, you can reduce the amount of Scotch bonnet you use slightly.

Red palm oil [9]

Red palm oil comes from cold-pressing the palm's red fruits (rather than just the kernels), and has a delicious earthy flavour and warm orange colour. Despite producing more palm oil than any other African country, Nigeria still has to import it because demand is so high. Most Nigerian palm oil comes from small local farms – nothing like the huge and damaging plantations in other parts of the world. Even so, always use a certified sustainable (RSPO) brand.

Plantain [10]

The plantain (boli in Yorùbá) is one of West Africa's favourite fruits. You can tell its ripeness from its colour: green (unripe) to yellow with small black blotches (ripe) to almost completely black (overripe). I use all kinds. Their natural sugars develop as they ripen, a process you can speed up by sealing them in a bag with an apple overnight. Green plantain is great for crisps (p.106) and fries, while yellow to black is best for sweeter items, such as dodo (p.99), brownies (p.138) and even arancini (p.88). You may feel tempted to substitute plantains with bananas; definitely resist that urge.

Maggi seasoning cubes [11]

Wrapped in blazing gold and red foil, these spicy stock cubes are beloved throughout Nigeria, and widely considered absolute essentials for creating explosively flavoursome savoury rice, stews and sauces, including jollof (p.48), groundnut stew (p.36) and ata dindin (p.133).

Hickory smoke powder [12]

The most delicious Nigerian food is roasted outside over an open fire. But using this, or liquid smoke, is the next best thing to get that deep smoky flavour. It's not a staple of Nigerian cooking, but it is of mine!

SOUPS, STEWS & SWALLOWS

Swallows

'Swallows' is a general term for a soft starchy dough, typically made by boiling pounded or floured plantains, cassava, yams or a combination thereof. They're used as a kind of edible utensil to eat soups and stews. You pinch off a small piece, roll it into a ball with your palm and make a dimple with your thumb, then scoop up the food and eat both together. When preparing, the dough should form a malleable ball inside your pot. Store swallows in the fridge, wrapped in clingfilm.

Àmàlà [1]

A classic Yorùbá swallow made from green plantain flour, cassava flour or yam flour (known as elubo). Use 2 parts water to 1 part sifted flour. Boil the water, add the flour and simmer rapidly while stirring continuously for 2 minutes. Add a splash of hot water, turn the heat down, stir for another 2 minutes, then stir *very* well for a final 2 minutes. Mould into tangerine-sized balls.

Iyan/Pounded Yam [2]

Peel, chunk and season 1kg/2lb 3oz puna yam, and boil it for 30 minutes. Drain and blend, then mash in a large bowl until smooth, sticky and slightly elastic. Soften with a splash of water, and with oiled hands, roll into tangerine-sized balls.

Tuwo shinkafa [3]

A rice swallow from northern Nigeria. It can be smooth using rice flour, or with more texture as in this version. Rinse 500g/1lb 2oz short-grain rice, then boil for 20 minutes until completely soft. Add a pinch of salt and mash with a wooden spoon or blend. Cook over a low heat for a few minutes until sticky. Leave to cool a little, and using wet hands, roll into tangerine-sized balls.

Èbà [4, 5, 6]

Made from garri, granules of cooked cassava; you can use either white garri [4], yellow garri [5] or Ijebu garri [6], which is slightly finer. Use 1 part garri to 3 parts water. Boil the water, add the garri and simmer rapidly, stirring hard (if your arm doesn't hurt, you can do more!) to bring it together. If still soft, add a touch more garri. Cool and roll into tangerine-sized balls. Wrap in clingfilm and firm up in the fridge.

Vegetable èbà [7, 8, 9]

A plant-based alternative to carb-rich traditional swallows. Blend 500g/1lb 2oz of either spinach [7], carrots [8], red cabbage [9], sweet potato, cauliflower, peppers or broccoli in a blender or food processor. Season and add 1 teaspoon of garlic granules. Simmer the blended vegetables for 3–5 minutes, stirring frequently. Add 260g/9¼oz garri in small increments, stirring continuously. Pour in 200ml/6¾fl oz hot water, lower the heat and stir for 2 minutes (adding hot water or garri to get the right texture). Mould as with normal èbà.

Ọbẹ̀ Ata
(Pepper Stew)

Serves 6 | 1 hour 35 minutes

This bright crimson, velvety pepper stew, comes in many guises back home. It's a real do-it-all, used as the base in many recipes – yes, typically meat stews – and is popular in Nigerian bukkas (street food stalls). It's sometimes even cooked down to a thick condiment (p.133). But to my mind, it can't be beaten paired with mushrooms, kale and aubergine; sweet potato and fried tofu are also excellent. It's a stew to eat with your hands using swallows, such as pounded yam or ẹ̀bà as pictured here (recipes on p.29), but you'll still win smiles serving it with rice.

105ml/3½fl oz vegetable oil

1 red onion, roughly chopped

3 red peppers, roughly chopped

1 Scotch bonnet (to taste), roughly chopped

4 large plum tomatoes, roughly chopped

2 tsp curry powder

1 tsp turmeric

2 tbsp dried thyme

1½ tsp fine salt

1 tsp freshly ground black pepper

450ml/¾ pint vegetable stock

1½ tbsp sustainable red palm oil

1 large aubergine, cut into 4cm/1½in chunks

250g/9oz oyster or button mushrooms, thickly sliced

150g/5oz kale (or spinach)

handful of chopped chives

Heat 60ml/2fl oz of the vegetable oil in a large casserole dish over a medium-high heat. Tip in the onion and red peppers and cook for 10 minutes, until the onion turns golden. Add the Scotch bonnet and tomatoes and cook for 8 minutes more. Then add the curry powder, turmeric, thyme, salt and pepper and cook for another few minutes, stirring well. Add the vegetable stock, then leave to cool a little.

Transfer the stew to a blender or food processor and blitz until completely smooth. Then tip it back into the casserole dish and bring to a simmer. Cover and cook for 30 minutes, stirring now and then. Stir in the red palm oil and cook for a further 10 minutes.

Meanwhile, heat 2 tablespoons of the vegetable oil in a wide frying pan over a medium-high heat and fry the aubergine for 5 minutes, turning regularly. Add the mushrooms and the remaining tablespoon of oil and cook for another 5 minutes, stirring, until everything is golden and softened, adding a big pinch of salt at the end of cooking. Set aside.

Destem and chop the kale and tip it into the stew, then cover and cook for 5-10 minutes, until wilting. Gently stir in the aubergine and mushrooms. Serve warm in bowls, scattered with the chopped chives.

Miyan Wake (Honey Bean Soup)

Serves 5 | 1 hour

Miyan wake is a bean soup enjoyed by the Hausa people in northern Nigeria, but in its various forms – the Yorùbá, for example, serve it as a smoother soup called gbegiri – it's loved throughout the country. The Hausa usually serve it with tuwo shinkafa (as pictured here, with recipe on p.29; soft balls of sticky short-grain rice, used to mop up the soup). If you can't find honey beans, black-eyed beans will do, but the soup's colour will be completely different; and irú (fermented locust beans) can be swapped out for miso or fermented black beans.

200g/7oz Nigerian honey beans (oloyin)

500g/1lb 2oz sweet potatoes, peeled

1 tsp potash (optional)

1 tbsp irú, soaked for 10 minutes

3 red or yellow peppers, diced

2 red onions, diced

3 garlic cloves, minced

7½cm/3in fresh ginger, peeled and grated

1½ tbsp sustainable red palm oil

1½ tsp fine salt

1 tsp freshly ground black pepper

1 vegetable stock cube, crumbled

2 spring onions, sliced diagonally

red pepper flakes, to garnish

Remove the bean skins according to the instructions on p.94.

Boil 600ml/1 pint water in a large pot, add the skinned beans and reduce to a simmer. Cover and cook the beans for 25 minutes, or until softened. Meanwhile, cut the sweet potatoes into 2cm/¾in chunks and place in a saucepan. Cover with boiling, salted water and boil for 10 minutes, then drain and set aside.

Once the beans are done, drain, allow to cool slightly, then mash or blend them to a purée. Add the potash, if using. Put the irú, one of the red or yellow peppers, one of the onions, all of the garlic and the ginger into a blender or food processor and blitz together, then add the mixture to the bean purée. Set aside.

Heat the red palm oil in a large pot over a medium heat. Add the remaining onion and red or yellow peppers and cook for 5–7 minutes. Then add the salt, pepper and stock cube along with the drained, parboiled sweet potatoes, the bean purée and 700ml/1¼ pints boiling water. Cook over a medium heat for 15 minutes, adding more water if it gets too dry.

Serve garnished with the sliced spring onions and a sprinkling of red pepper flakes. If reheating the soup, stir in a splash of warm water to loosen it.

Groundnut Stew
with Sweet Potato

Serves 6 | 1 hour 15 minutes

My mom doesn't cook - except for this. And, boy, does she cook it well. We ate this spicy ground-nut (the word Nigerians use for peanut) stew all the time as kids and never tired of it. Enjoyed throughout West Africa as 'mafé', and usually made with chicken, it has an unequalled palette of flavours: sweet tomatoes, aromatic cumin, smooth peanut butter and fiery Scotch bonnets, tempered with creamy coconut. Serve with brown rice as pictured here, èbà (p.29) or just as it is.

3 tbsp groundnut oil

1 white onion, finely chopped

1 or 2 Scotch bonnets (to taste)

2 tbsp fresh ginger, peeled and finely grated

4 garlic cloves, crushed

2 tsp ground cumin

1 tsp cayenne pepper

1 tsp ground white pepper

2 tbsp tomato purée

400g/14oz can chopped tomatoes

1kg/2lb 3oz sweet potatoes, peeled and cut into 3cm/1in chunks

180g/6¼oz smooth natural peanut butter

1 tsp fine salt

1 vegetable stock cube (preferably Maggi), crumbled

150g/5oz unsalted peanuts

250g/9oz fresh spinach, washed

160ml/5½fl oz coconut cream

3 limes (1 juiced, 2 to garnish)

Heat the oil (red palm or vegetable oil work too) in a large pan, over a medium heat. Brown the onion for about 10 minutes, stirring occasionally. Meanwhile deseed and finely chop the Scotch bonnets, then add them to the pan along with the ginger. Cook for 2 minutes, then add the garlic, stirring for another minute. Tip in the cumin, cayenne pepper and white pepper and cook for 1 minute more, stirring to avoid any burning.

Stir in the tomato purée, then add the tomatoes, sweet pota-toes, peanut butter, salt and stock cube with 1 litre/1¾ pints boiling water. Bring to the boil, before reducing to a simmer. Cover the pot three-quarters with a lid and cook for 50 minutes, stirring occasionally.

Meanwhile, preheat your oven to 180°C/350°F (160°C/325°F fan) for the roast peanut topping. Blitz the peanuts in a food processor for just a few seconds, so you still have chunks and a variation of textures. Spread them out on a tray and bake in the centre of the oven for about 15 minutes, or until dark brown in colour, before setting aside.

When the stew's had its 50 minutes, mash a few of the sweet potatoes, leaving some chunks, and stir in the spinach, coconut cream and lime juice.

Serve topped with the oven-roasted peanuts and the remaining limes, cut into wedges. Crispy onions, crushed plantain crisps (p.106) or chilli flakes, for extra heat, also garnish well.

Ọbẹ̀ kìí gbé inú àgbà mì

Soup does not move around
in an elder's belly

Ẹ̀fọ́ Riro
(Stewed Greens)

Serves 4 | 1 hour 30 minutes

Ẹ̀fọ́ riro is a stew of leafy greens with a rich tomato and pepper base. Whether it's traditional ẹ̀fọ́ shoko (Lagos spinach) or spinach and kale from your local supermarket, any greens are good for this hearty, healthy meal. The flavour that leaves you wanting more comes from the irú (fermented locust beans), which you can substitute for miso, tahini, or even just by upping the vegetable stock. Pictured here with red cabbage ẹ̀bà (p.29), this stew is also great served with àmàlà or iyan/pounded yam (recipes for both are also on p.29), wild rice or semolina.

3 red peppers

1½ red onions

2 large plum tomatoes

3 garlic cloves

1 Scotch bonnet (to taste)

7½cm/3in fresh ginger, peeled

1½ tsp fine salt

4 tbsp sustainable red palm oil

400g/14oz greens, such as spinach, chopped kale or collard greens

1 tbsp irú, soaked for 10 minutes

1 tsp dried thyme

1 tsp ground cumin

1 tsp curry powder

1½ tsp ground turmeric

1 tsp ground white pepper

1 vegetable stock cube, dissolved in 150ml/5fl oz water

250g/9oz button mushrooms, halved

Start by making your base. Roughly chop 2 of the red peppers, 1 onion, the tomatoes, garlic and Scotch bonnet and finely chop the ginger, then add all to a blender or food processor with ½ a teaspoon of the salt. Blend until smooth. Heat 3 tablespoons of the oil in a wide saucepan over a medium-high heat, then tip in the blended ingredients. Let the mixture bubble, then reduce the heat. Cover and cook for 30 minutes, stirring occasionally to make sure it doesn't burn while it reduces.

Meanwhile, blanch your greens. Boil a large pot of water and place a bowl of cold water beside it. Dunk the greens in the boiling water for 1 minute. Transfer to the cold water with a slotted spoon to halt the cooking process. (You may need to do this in batches.) Drain again, shake and pat dry.

Rinse the pot, add the remaining tablespoon of oil and place over a medium-high heat. Finely chop the remaining ½ an onion and roughly chop the last red pepper, then add both to the pot and cook for 8 minutes. Stir in the irú, thyme, all the spices, 1 teaspoon of salt and the pepper and cook for 2-3 minutes, then pour in the stock. Next, carefully tip in the base from earlier, reduce the heat and leave to cook for 15 minutes.

Stir in the mushrooms and continue cooking for 5 minutes, then add the greens in batches, stirring them in, and cook for another 5 minutes. Season to taste if needed, then serve.

Frejon
(Coconut and Bean Soup)

Serves 4-6 | 2 hours 45 minutes

We used to spend most Easters with our friends, the Johnsons, who always served frejon, perfuming the air with cloves and spice. In Lagos, this thick, almost pasty, Brazilian delicacy is served on Good Friday with lots of fish and garri. My version is far soupier, dressed with crunchy toppings, and can be enjoyed any day of the year.

450g/1lb dried black beans

7 whole cloves, tied in a muslin

2 garlic cloves, minced

400ml/13½fl oz can full-fat coconut milk

50g/2oz caster sugar

½ tsp ground ginger

1 tsp fine salt

The toppings

2 green peppers, finely diced

drizzle of vegetable oil

2 tbsp garri, per serving

1 tbsp coconut cream, per serving

3 spring onions, sliced diagonally

pinch of chilli flakes, per serving

small handful of coriander

Wash the black beans and place them in a large saucepan, covered with plenty of water. Add the tied-up cloves. Bring to the boil, and simmer for 1–1½ hours, until the beans are soft. Check intermittently, topping up with water if needed.

Take off the heat and allow to cool a little, setting aside the tied-up cloves for later. Drain the beans through a sieve set over a large bowl, to reserve the cooking water. Check the volume of cooking water you have and top up to 400ml/13½fl oz, with more water, if you need to. Tip the beans, cooking water, garlic and coconut milk into a blender or food processor, and pulse until completely smooth. Pass the mixture through a fine sieve.

Return the mixture to the pan. Stir through the sugar, ginger and salt, then add the reserved, tied-up cloves. Bring to a gentle simmer, cover, and cook for 40 minutes–1 hour, stirring regularly to stop the mixture from catching, until it thickens like a custard. (Add a little water if it becomes too thick, or before reheating.)

Preheat your oven to 200°C/400°F (180°C/350°F fan). Toss the green peppers in oil, spread them out across an oven tray, and season. Roast in the oven for 20–25 minutes, stirring halfway through. Meanwhile, place the garri in a dry frying pan over a medium heat and cook for 1–2 minutes, stirring, until toasted.

Divide the frejon into bowls and serve straight away, topped with the coconut cream, toasted garri, some roasted green pepper, a sprinkling of spring onions, the chilli flakes and a few coriander leaves.

MAINS

Asaro-Stuffed Sweet Potatoes

Serves 6 | 1 hour 15 minutes

Asaro is a Yorùbá pottage (a thick stew) made from yams with a creamy base of peppers and tomato. I adore it scooped into roasted sweet-potato skins and finished with cool coconut yoghurt, pomegranate seeds, fresh coriander and wedges of lime. And you can never have too many crispy shallots to pile on top.

6 large sweet potatoes

4 medium shallots, peeled and thinly sliced

pinch of sea salt

50ml/1¾fl oz vegetable oil

4 garlic cloves, crushed

7½cm/3in fresh ginger, peeled and grated

1 Scotch bonnet (to taste), minced

2½ tsp ground turmeric

1 vegetable stock cube, crumbled

1 tsp fine salt

2 tbsp tomato purée

2 red peppers

400g/14oz can chopped tomatoes

500g/1lb 2oz puna yam (about half a tuber), peeled and diced

1 tbsp sustainable red palm oil (or vegetable oil)

400ml/13½fl oz can full-fat coconut milk

200g/7oz kale, shredded

100g/3½oz coconut yoghurt

Preheat the oven to 200°C/400°F (180°C/350°F fan). Prick the sweet potatoes all over, season and bake on a greased tray for 1 hour or until soft.

Meanwhile, fry the shallots in the vegetable oil in a large pan over a medium-high heat for about 15 minutes, or until golden and crispy, stirring occasionally. Use a slotted spoon to transfer the shallots to a plate lined with kitchen paper, sprinkle with the sea salt and set aside.

Cook the garlic and ginger in the same oil for 1 minute. Add the Scotch bonnet, turmeric, stock cube, fine salt and tomato purée, stirring for a few minutes. Put the red peppers in a blender or food processor and blitz until smooth, then add them to the pan with the chopped tomatoes and cook for 10 minutes more.

Pour in 500ml/1 pint boiling water and bring everything to the boil, then reduce to a simmer and add the diced yam. Cover and cook for 30 minutes, stirring occasionally.

When the sweet potatoes are done, halve them lengthways and scoop out the flesh, lightly mashing it into the stew. Set the skins aside. Add the palm oil and coconut milk to the stew and simmer, uncovered, for 8 minutes. Stir in the kale and cook for another 4–5 minutes before removing from the heat.

Spoon the stew into the sweet potato skins, then top each with a tablespoon of the coconut yoghurt and a sprinkling of crispy shallots. You can garnish with pomegranate seeds, fresh coriander and lime wedges, if you like.

Classic Jollof

Serves 6–8 | 1 hour 30 minutes

Jollof rice is enjoyed all across West Africa and is one of the best-known African dishes around the world. It comes in many iterations, but this is the classic home-cooked Nigerian version, rich in tomatoes and fired by Scotch bonnets. Although it's an everyday favourite, on special occasions it comes as 'party rice', when the pot is overheated so that the bottom of the rice gently burns and infuses the rest with a distinctly sweet, smoky flavour. Tuck right in or serve jollof with ọbẹ ata (p.32), dodo (p.99), a cool coleslaw or lashings of chilli sauce (p.124 or p.133).

3 medium plum tomatoes (about 320g/11½oz)

1 red pepper

1 Scotch bonnet (to taste)

5 red onions

3 tbsp vegetable oil, plus more for drizzling

4 garlic cloves, crushed

7½cm/3in fresh ginger, peeled and finely chopped

1 tsp smoked paprika

1 tsp cayenne pepper

2½ tsp curry powder

1 tsp ground turmeric

1 vegetable stock cube (preferably Maggi), crumbled

Roughly chop the plum tomatoes, red pepper, Scotch bonnet and 1 red onion, then tip them into a blender or food processor and blitz until smooth. Set aside.

Heat the 3 tablespoons of oil in a medium sauté pan or casserole dish over a medium heat. Thinly slice 2 red onions and add them to the pan. Cook for 15 minutes until golden. Stir in the garlic and ginger and cook for 1 minute. Add the spices, stock cube, salt and pepper and cook for 1 minute more.

Squeeze in the tomato purée and add the liquid smoke, if using, then stir well. Add the blended tomato and pepper mixture. Bring to a simmer, then cover, leaving the lid slightly ajar, and cook for 20–25 minutes until thickened, stirring occasionally to make sure it doesn't burn.

Meanwhile, parboil the rice. First, rinse it really well in a sieve until the water runs almost clear, then cover generously with boiling water in a saucepan. Bring to the boil, cover and simmer for no more than 5 minutes; it should still be really firm. Drain the rice and set aside.

2 tsp fine salt

1 tsp freshly ground black pepper

2 tbsp tomato purée

1 tbsp liquid smoke (optional)

400g/14oz long-grain rice

3 tbsp fresh thyme leaves
(or 1 tbsp dried)

2 bay leaves

small handful of fresh thyme
sprigs

12 baby plum tomatoes
on the vine

When the sauce has had its time, add the parboiled rice and the thyme and bay leaves, then stir well. Cover the pot with aluminium foil to seal in the flavour, pop on the lid and cook for 20 minutes until all the sauce has been absorbed. Resist the temptation to stir, as it can make the rice soggy; the bottom of the pot may crisp a little, but that's to be welcomed (see 'party rice' below).

Preheat the oven to 200°C/400°F (180°C/350°F fan). Heat a drizzle of oil in a frying pan, thinly slice the 2 remaining onions and add to the pan. Cook for 5–10 minutes, until softened but with a little crunch. Season and stir through a few of the thyme sprigs, then set aside.

Put the baby plum tomatoes on a small baking tray, drizzle with oil and season, then roast in the oven for 10–15 minutes, until just starting to burst.

When the rice is ready, remove it from the heat and let it sit (without stirring) for at least 10 minutes, fully covered. Then fluff lightly with a fork. Serve garnished with the softened onions, roasted tomatoes and some more thyme sprigs.

Party rice

To get the sweet and smoky flavour of 'party rice', turn the heat up high towards the end of cooking, leaving the lid on and the flavour sealed in. Let the bottom of the rice slightly burn for up to 5 minutes before leaving it to sit. The scorched rice at the bottom is called 'bottom pot' or kanzo, and it's the best part.

Fonio Tabbouleh

Serves 5 | 35 minutes

It's a mystery to me why fonio (sometimes known as 'acha' or 'acca' on the street), a gluten-free millet that has been cultivated in West Africa for over 5000 years, hasn't already become the West's next superfood. Light, fluffy and with a signature nutty flavour, it's packed to the brim with nutrients. The Lebanese community I grew up with in Nigeria rightly recruited it above alternatives bulgur or couscous for their tabbouleh, the incredibly refreshing parsley salad that's so delicious for lunch on hot days or as part of a larger sharing platter.

100g/3½oz fonio (or bulgur or couscous)

½ tsp fine salt

1 cucumber

300g/10½oz curly parsley

1 red onion

1 large red pepper

3 medium tomatoes

lemon slices, to garnish

handful of fresh mint leaves, to garnish

The dressing

2 garlic cloves, minced

2 lemons, zested and juiced

100ml/3½fl oz extra virgin olive oil

1 tsp ground coriander

¾ tsp ground cumin

½ tsp ground cardamom

½ tsp freshly ground black pepper

1 tsp fine salt

Put the fonio, 250ml/8½fl oz water and the salt into a saucepan. Bring to the boil, reduce the heat and cook for 2–3 minutes, until the water has been absorbed. Remove from the heat and fluff with a fork, then pop the lid on and set aside to cool for at least 10 minutes, allowing it to get tender.

Halve the cucumber and deseed it. Chop it up finely, along with the parsley, onion, red pepper and tomatoes. Drain away any excess juice, especially from the tomatoes, and give all the salad items a good toss in a large mixing bowl.

For the dressing, mix all the ingredients together in a jug.

Once the fonio has cooled, stir it into the salad mix. Drizzle the dressing over and toss to coat until it's nice and glossy. Season to taste, garnish with a couple of lemon slices and the mint leaves, then serve fresh.

Cassava and Beetroot Gnocchi

Serves 4 | 2 hours 10 minutes

My best friend, who also happens to be my twin brother, Carl (or Baba Garri as we sometimes call him), has a beautiful cassava farm deep in Oyo state. This recipe came about to help him promote his gluten-free cassava flour. It's an amazingly versatile ingredient, and just sour enough to make the tastebuds sing. It combines brilliantly with beetroot and sweet potato to make pillowy gnocchi, which is best served fresh with lots and lots of garlicky brown butter, crispy sage and lemon zest.

The gnocchi

500g/1lb 2oz beetroot

1½ tbsp olive oil

325g/11½oz sweet potato

200g/7oz cassava flour, plus more for dusting

½ tsp ground nutmeg

1 tsp fine salt

½ tsp freshly ground black pepper

Preheat the oven to 200°C/400°F (180°C/350°F fan). Place the beetroot in a roasting dish. Drizzle with the oil and sprinkle with a little salt. Pour 125ml/4¼fl oz water into the dish and cover tightly with aluminium foil. Prick the sweet potato all over and place on a baking tray. Put the potato and beetroot into the oven and roast for 1 hour.

Pierce the potato and beetroot with a knife to check they're cooked all the way through. If not, return to the oven for another 15 minutes and check again. Once cooked, remove the skin from the potato and mash the flesh in a medium bowl. Peel the beetroot, using gloves if they're still very hot. Chop roughly, and blitz in a blender or food processor until smooth.

Add the beetroot to the bowl with the sweet potato, along with the cassava flour, nutmeg, salt and pepper. Combine well into a dough, using your hands. If it's too sticky to be manageable, add a little more cassava flour. Transfer the dough onto a surface lightly dusted with cassava flour and flatten with a rolling pin until it's about 2½cm/1in thick. Line a baking tray with baking parchment.

The sauce

150g/5oz protein-rich vegan butter (e.g. soy), unsalted

16 fresh sage leaves

pinch of fine salt

2 garlic cloves, crushed

2 heaped tbsp pine nuts, toasted

2 tbsp finely grated lemon zest

1 tbsp grated vegan parmesan

Lightly dust the dough and a sharp knife with cassava flour again; this helps to stop it sticking and absorbs any excess water. Cut the dough into 2cm/¾in-thick strips using the dusted knife. Roll the strips into long snakes about 1½cm/½in thick and slice into 2cm/¾in pieces, again using a dusted knife. Put the gnocchi in the tray as you go.

To cook the gnocchi, bring a large pot of salted water to the boil. Add the gnocchi in batches, so as to not overcrowd the pot, for about 3 minutes each or until the gnocchi floats to the surface. It's a good idea to use a timer, as the water will be red and cloudy, making the gnocchi difficult to spot. Remove the gnocchi using a slotted spoon and transfer to an oiled tray. Don't stack them over each other as they will stick.

Melt the butter in a wide frying pan over a medium-high heat. Add the sage leaves and the pinch of salt and cook for about 5 minutes, until the sage has darkened in colour and the butter has browned; low-protein butters won't brown properly. Remove the sage to use as a garnish when serving.

Add the garlic to the pan and let it sizzle, then tip in the gnocchi and fry for about 3 minutes. Remove from the heat and add the toasted pine nuts and most of the lemon zest and parmesan. Season if needed. Make sure the gnocchi is well coated in the sauce, then top with the darkened sage and the rest of the parmesan and lemon zest. Serve warm.

Lebanese-Nigerian Roast Chickpea Shawarma

Serves 6 (12 wraps) | 50 minutes, not including flatbreads

It's 2 a.m. in Lagos and you've had a few drinks. This is exactly what's needed to set you straight, believe me – and so much better than the beef and chicken shawarmas you usually find. There's something so wholesome and healing about the crisped chickpeas and crunchy vegetables, slathered in an eye-opening lemon-tahini sauce, all bundled up in beetroot flatbread wraps. It gives an instant boost – and soaks up all those cocktails, too!

2 × 400g/14oz cans chickpeas

2 tbsp olive oil

2 tsp ground coriander

2 tsp smoked paprika

½ tsp ground ginger

1 tsp ground cumin

½ tsp ground cinnamon

½ tsp ground cayenne pepper

1 tsp fine salt

1 tsp freshly ground black pepper

The tahini sauce

3 small garlic cloves

1½ tbsp dill

110g/4oz tahini

5 tbsp dairy-free milk

¾ tbsp extra virgin olive oil

2½ tbsp lemon juice

¾ tsp fine salt

¼ tsp freshly ground black pepper

Preheat the oven to 200°C/400°F (180°C/350°F fan) and line an oven tray with baking parchment. Rinse and drain the chickpeas.

Combine the olive oil, coriander, paprika, ginger, cumin, cinnamon, cayenne pepper, salt and black pepper in a medium bowl. Tip in the chickpeas and toss until they have a thick, even coating. Empty them onto the tray and roast for 20 minutes, stirring every 5–10 minutes. Remove from the oven and leave to cool.

To make the tahini sauce, peel and crush the garlic cloves and finely chop the dill, then add them with the rest of the sauce ingredients to a blender or food processor. Blitz until smooth. Pour the sauce into a bowl for later. You can add another tablespoon of dairy-free milk to loosen it before using, if needed.

Next, prepare your salad. Finely shred the cabbage, carrots and cucumber, halve the tomatoes and finely slice the red onion. Add everything to a medium bowl, toss, and set aside.

The salad and wraps

½ red cabbage

2 medium carrots

½ cucumber or 1 Persian cucumber

12 cherry tomatoes

1 red onion

12 beetroot flatbreads (p.104)

Assemble the shawarma by spreading some tahini sauce on each of the (ideally) warm, fresh flatbreads. Then top them with some of the salad, roasted chickpeas and more tahini sauce. Fresh mint leaves and chilli sauce (like ata dindin, p.133) also make great garnishes.

Roll up the bread, tuck in the edges and serve. To make the shawarma easier to hold, you can wrap them in aluminium foil or paper napkins, tied with string or pierced with toothpicks to keep them secure.

Yellow Rice

Serves 8 | 50 minutes

This iconic, yellow, crispy, caramelly Nigerian rice is best served hot, loaded with dodo (p.99) and lashings of spicy ata dindin (p.133) or alongside your favourite stew. Usually made with chopped beef liver, this version features an array of vegetables paired with aromatic herbs and spices. Caribbean-blend curry powders work best for this recipe and if you can't find shombo peppers, you can also use jalapeño or serrano peppers.

500g/1lb 2oz long-grain rice

4 tbsp vegetable oil

1 red onion, diced

3 garlic cloves

1 or 2 shombo (cayenne) peppers

3 large flat mushrooms

3 medium carrots, peeled

2 yellow, orange or green peppers

150g/5oz green beans

sprig of fresh rosemary

2 tsp dried thyme

2 bay leaves

1½ tsp turmeric powder

2 tsp curry powder

1 tsp ground ginger

1 tsp ehuru (calabash nutmeg) or ground nutmeg

2 tsp fine salt

1 tsp freshly ground black pepper

500ml/1 pint vegetable stock

150g/5oz fresh shelled peas

200g/7oz can sweetcorn, drained

Gently stir the rice in water to remove the starch, then drain and repeat until the water stays clear.

Heat the oil in a casserole dish over a medium heat. Add the red onion and cook for about 10 minutes until golden.

Meanwhile, finely chop the garlic and shombo peppers, dice the mushrooms, carrots and deseeded yellow, orange or green peppers, and trim and chop the green beans. Add them all to the pot, stir, and cook for 5 minutes. Add the rosemary sprig, thyme, bay leaves, all the spices and the salt and pepper. Mix and cook for 2–3 minutes, then gently stir the rice into the pan in small increments, cooking for 2 minutes more.

Slowly pour in the vegetable stock, bring it to a boil and then reduce to a simmer. Give it one good stir, then cover and cook gently until the rice has absorbed the stock, roughly 10 minutes. Monitor it but try not to stir. If needed, add a small splash of hot water.

Add the peas and sweetcorn, return the lid, and cook for a further 3-5 minutes, until the peas are tender. Remove from the heat and leave to sit for 10 minutes. Remove the bay leaves, and lightly fluff the rice with a fork. You could garnish with crispy onions, chilli sauce and plenty of fresh, chopped parsley.

Àjoje ló má n dun

Eating together is what makes
the meal special

Mango Salad

Serves 6-8 | 30 minutes

There's so much brightness and freshness to this salad. Packed with punchy flavours led by the mango, it's streaked with pomegranate molasses and seeds, and topped off with candied peanuts and a sugar-spice dressing, to give sweetness throughout. But with sharp citrus cutting through and the satisfyingly wholesome crunch of raw vegetables and lettuce leaves, it's truly a fulfilling meal in itself – even though it pairs beautifully with any savoury dish in this book.

3 mangoes, diced

2 medium avocados, peeled, destoned and diced

1 red pepper, finely diced

½ red onion, thinly sliced

1 round lettuce, roughly chopped

100g/3½oz pomegranate seeds

handful of fresh coriander and mint, chopped

2½ tbsp pomegranate molasses

1 lime, to garnish

The candied peanuts

100g/3½oz unsalted peanuts

60g/2¼oz light brown sugar

sprinkling of chilli powder

pinch of fine salt

The dressing

40ml/1¼fl oz avocado oil

2 limes, zested and juiced

2 garlic cloves, minced

1 tsp ground cumin

2 tsp light brown sugar

large pinch of fine salt

large pinch of chilli flakes

Start with the candied peanuts. Roughly crush the peanuts using a rolling pin (you can do this while they are still in the bag, if you wish). Combine them with the other candied peanuts ingredients and 25ml/¾fl oz water in a wide frying pan over a medium heat. Keep stirring until the peanuts caramelise and turn brown, thick and sticky. Remove before they burn. Tip the peanuts onto a lined or greased tray and spread them out as much as you can to make sure they don't clump together. Leave to cool.

For the dressing, put all the ingredients in a small jug and mix well. (If you can't find avocado oil, vegetable oil will do.)

When ready to serve, put the mango, avocado, red pepper, onion, lettuce, pomegranate seeds and herbs in a large bowl. Toss gently to mix. Spatter the pomegranate molasses across the top.

Drizzle the dressing over the salad and scatter the peanuts evenly across its surface. Serve fresh, garnished with the lime, cut into wedges. If you like, add a scattering of chilli flakes for more heat.

Jollof Quinoa Stuffed Peppers

Serves 4 | 2 hours

If it isn't already abundantly clear from its prominence in this book, I *really* like jollof. Usually, jollof is made with its world-famous base of red pepper, tomato and onion, but this jollof recipe is extra tomatoey, with the red pepper element only coming into the roasting of the dish at the very end. It's a supremely good foil for eccentric garnishing; the pomegranate molasses may sound strange, but it adds a fruity tang that intensifies the rich tomato flavour of the quinoa. Pick and choose which garnishes serve you best, but I highly recommend drenching this dish in coconut yoghurt. If you'd like a quicker meal, or something to stash in the fridge for speedy weekday lunches, forgo the red peppers and roasting, and you can fill up on a bowl of straight-up jollof quinoa (with all, or none, of the toppings) in under an hour.

3½ tbsp vegetable oil, plus more for drizzling

1 red onion (½ finely sliced, ½ roughly chopped)

2 garlic cloves, minced

7½cm/3in fresh ginger, peeled and grated

1 Scotch bonnet (to taste), roughly chopped

1 tbsp fresh thyme leaves

400g/14oz can chopped tomatoes

1 tbsp of tomato purée

2 tsp liquid smoke

2 tsp smoked paprika

½ tsp ground nutmeg

½ tsp ground cloves

1 vegetable stock cube, crumbled

Pour 2½ tablespoons of the vegetable oil into a medium-sized pot and place over a medium heat. Sauté the sliced onion for 8–10 minutes until golden. Then add the garlic, ginger, Scotch bonnet and thyme and cook for 2 minutes.

Add the chopped red onion, canned tomatoes and tomato purée to a blender or food processor and blitz until smooth. Add the mixture to the pot, cover and leave to cook for 20 minutes. Stir in the liquid smoke, paprika, nutmeg, ground cloves, vegetable stock cube, salt and pepper and cook for 2–3 minutes. Tip in the quinoa, followed by 400ml/13½fl oz boiling water. Bring it back to the boil, then turn down the heat, cover, and simmer for 20–30 minutes or until the quinoa is cooked (adding more water if needed). Remove it from the heat and fluff with a fork.

Preheat your oven to 190°C/375°F (170°C/340°F fan) and line a baking tray with baking parchment. Brush the red pepper halves with the remaining tablespoon of oil and sprinkle with a pinch of salt. Stuff the peppers with the quinoa, then cover with some lightly oiled aluminium foil and place in the oven for

1 tsp fine salt

1 tsp freshly ground black pepper

200g/7oz quinoa, washed and drained

4 red peppers, deseeded and halved lengthways

To serve

coconut yoghurt

pomegranate molasses

finely sliced spring onion

handful of fresh thyme sprigs

35–45 minutes, until the peppers are tender. Remove the foil, drizzle with a little oil and return to the oven for 5–10 minutes more to give the quinoa a nice crunchy topping.

Serve warm, topped with some coconut yoghurt, pomegranate molasses, sliced spring onion and fresh thyme sprigs. Other great garnishes include finely grated vegan parmesan, diced red onion and ata dindin (p.133).

Avocado Plantain Salad

Serves 4-6 | 35 minutes

If you ever needed something to dispel the clouds on a grey day, this salad is surely it. Not only is it a sunny burst of flavours – caramelly plantain mixed with punchy, lime-pickled red onion and smooth avocado – its vivid colours seem to jump right out of the bowl. Cauliflower comes naturally in a variety of hues (green, white, orange and purple); so feel free to be creative with the one you choose. On its own, it's a truly nutritious bowl of goodness, but it makes a handsome accompaniment to larger feasts, too.

1 red onion, finely sliced

1 lime, juiced

pinch of fine salt

200g/7oz cauliflower, cut into small florets

2½ tbsp vegetable oil

2 yellow plantains

1 medium red pepper, cut into 2cm/¾in dice

2 medium avocados, peeled, destoned and cut into chunks

large handful of fresh coriander, leaves picked and roughly chopped

Preheat the oven to 200°C/400°F (180°C/350°F fan). Mix the onion and lime juice in a small bowl, add the pinch of salt and set aside to pickle.

Tip the cauliflower onto a baking tray, drizzle with 1 tablespoon of the vegetable oil, season and toss to combine. Roast for 20 minutes until tender, stirring halfway through, and set aside.

Meanwhile, top and tail the plantain, then slice in half lengthways and peel. Cut the flesh into 2–2½cm/¾–1in pieces.

Heat the remaining oil in a large frying pan over a medium-high heat. Add your plantain and red pepper to the pan, and sauté for 10 minutes, or until the plantains are deep caramel in colour and the peppers are tender. Season and set aside.

When everything's ready, bring together the plantain, red pepper, roasted cauliflower and avocado in a large bowl. Top with the coriander and pickled red onion and toss to combine. Serve fresh.

Coconut Rice

Serves 6 | 1 hour

'There is rice at home,' is a phrase many Nigerians have a love-hate relationship with. It can mean, 'Be thankful for the tasty food we have!' But it can also mean, 'No, we are not going out! There's always rice at home.' It's also a reminder that rice, although humble, is as homely, comforting and reliable as any meal. For those of us living abroad, it's a bridge back home. This dish goes well with pretty much any stew, but feel free to gorge on it straight from the pot with lots of lime and chilli sauce.

400g/14oz jasmine rice

1 red onion, finely diced

2½ tbsp coconut oil

2 garlic cloves, crushed

1½cm/½in ginger, peeled and finely chopped

2 red peppers, deseeded and diced

1 Scotch bonnet, deseeded and diced

1 bay leaf

1 tsp curry powder

1½ tsp dried thyme

1 tsp nutmeg

1 tsp fine salt

260g/9¼oz can full-fat coconut milk

260ml/8¾fl oz vegetable stock

1 tbsp sugar (optional)

½ small red cabbage

Gently stir the rice in water to remove the starch, then drain and repeat until the water stays clear.

Sauté the onion in the coconut oil in a large pan over a medium-high heat for 10 minutes. Add the garlic, ginger, red peppers and Scotch bonnet and cook for a further 2 minutes. Stir in the bay leaf, curry powder, thyme, nutmeg and salt.

Pour in the coconut milk and stock (and add the sugar if you want to sweeten the rice). Bring to the boil, then tip in the rice. Cover and turn down to a rapid simmer, leaving to cook for 15 minutes.

Meanwhile, finely shred the red cabbage; a mandolin helps. Reduce the heat again and place the red cabbage on top of the rice. Don't stir it in. Cook, covered, for a further 15 minutes.

Remove from the heat and let it sit (don't stir) for up to 10 minutes, then fluff, scraping any delicious crispy rice from the bottom of the pan (the best part!).

You could garnish, if you like, with some toasted coconut flakes, chilli flakes, lime zest, lime wedges for squeezing or chilli sauce.

Plantain Salad Imoyo

Serves 4 | 50 minutes, plus marinading time

Imoyo is a type of recipe that owes its distinctive style to the Brazilian heritage in Nigerian cuisine. These recipes typically use raw ingredients and citrus marinades, and often feature plantains, garlic and green peppers, too. I'm rarely one to have just a salad, but for me an imoyo salad is spicy-sweet enough to stand up for itself. I sometimes find myself adding more agave syrup to my bowl, especially if my plantains weren't ripe and sweet enough to balance the lingering burn of the Scotch bonnet and the tangy, salty dressing.

2 ripe yellow plantains (with black splotches)

1 tbsp vegetable oil

¼ tsp fine salt

1 cucumber, finely diced

1 green pepper, finely diced

30g/1oz fresh parsley, leaves picked and roughly chopped

1 avocado, peeled, destoned and diced (optional)

The dressing

3 tbsp lemon juice

4 tbsp extra virgin olive oil

1 tbsp agave syrup

1 Scotch bonnet (to taste), very finely chopped

2 garlic cloves, crushed

½ tsp fine salt

½ tsp freshly ground black pepper

Heat the oven to 180°C/350°F (160°C/325°F fan). Top and tail the plantains, then score the skin down the length of each, trying not to cut through to the flesh. Repeat down the opposite length and remove the skin, then cut the flesh into 1½cm/½in dice.

Tip them onto a large non-stick baking tray, drizzle with the oil, sprinkle with the salt and toss to coat. Spread across the tray so the pieces don't overlap, and roast for 30–35 minutes, or until golden and caramelised around the edges, stirring halfway through. Remove from the oven and set aside to cool.

Meanwhile, combine all the dressing ingredients in a small jug and give them a good stir.

Toss the cucumber, green pepper, parsley and cooled roasted plantain together in a large bowl. (Add the avocado, if using, too.) Pour the dressing over everything and give it a good mix. Put the salad in the fridge for 30 minutes, so the flavours have a chance to infuse, then serve.

Plantain-Bean Salsa Lettuce Boats

Serves 6 | 1 hour, plus soaking time

With so many opposing elements of flavour and texture thrown together, it's a wonder this dish works so well. But it does. Chilli heat, spicy beans, sweet soft plantain, crisp lettuce and tangy sour cream – it's pure stimulation for the tastebuds. You can also chop up the lettuce and serve the salsa in a large bowl, like a summery salad, or make it more substantial by swapping out the lettuce for beetroot flatbread (p.104).

300g/10½oz wholegrain rice

1 ripe yellow plantain

5 tbsp extra virgin olive oil

400g/14oz can black beans, rinsed and drained

1 medium red onion, finely diced

2 garlic cloves, crushed

2 medium avocados, peeled, destoned and diced

2 limes (1 zested and juiced, 1 juiced)

½ tsp red pepper flakes

¾ tsp chilli powder

1 tsp ground cumin

1 tsp ground cinnamon

1 tsp brown sugar

½ tsp fine salt

½ tsp freshly cracked black pepper

1 or 2 heads romaine (cos) lettuce, for 24 leaves

plantain crisps (p.106), to garnish

Boil the rice in salted water, according to the pack instructions. Meanwhile, line a plate with kitchen paper and set aside.

Top and tail the plantain. Draw a knife down the length of it, scoring the skin but trying not to cut through the flesh. Repeat down the opposite side and remove the skin, then finely dice. In a wide frying pan, heat 2 tablespoons of the olive oil over a medium-high heat. Add the plantain and cook for about 5 minutes until golden, then transfer to the lined plate.

Combine the black beans, onion, garlic and avocado in a medium-sized mixing bowl, then stir in the cooked plantain. In a small bowl, mix together the lime zest and juice, the remaining 3 tablespoons of olive oil and the red pepper flakes, chilli powder, cumin, cinnamon, brown sugar, salt and black pepper, and stir well. Add this to the plantain-bean mix, stir, and leave to sit for 20 minutes so the flavours can develop.

For the lime sour cream, add all of the ingredients to a blender or food processor and blend until smooth.

The lime sour cream

135g/4¾oz raw cashews,
soaked for 6 hours or overnight

125g/4½oz unsweetened,
non-dairy yoghurt

2 limes, juiced

1 tsp apple cider vinegar

¾ tsp fine salt

To serve, layer 2 lettuce leaves on top of each other to make one firm boat. You should have 12 boats in total. Spread them with a layer of the lime sour cream, then spoon in some rice and a generous helping of plantain salsa. Garnish with further dollops of the lime sour cream, then crush up the plantain crisps and sprinkle them over. You could also add chopped coriander or parsley, extra lime zest and lime wedges, if you like.

SIDES &
SNACKS

Suya-Battered Vegetable Kebabs

Serves 6 | 1 hour

After my dad finished work, my family would meet at the Ibadan polo club for a cold beer and a plate of suya: a spicy meat kebab, cooked over firewood and rubbed in suya spice (a traditional peanut-based spice mix, also called yaji). These veg kebabs take the idea further, upping the spice mix with extra roasted peanuts to make a crunchy coating. Ose oji, a spiced peanut butter sauce originating from the Igbo people in Nigeria, is the ideal accompaniment.

12 wooden skewers

300g/10½oz roasted unsalted peanuts

1½ tsp garlic powder

1 vegetable stock cube, crumbled

2 tsp cayenne pepper (to taste)

2 tsp paprika

2 tsp ground ginger

½ tsp ground cloves

½ tsp allspice

½ tsp ground nutmeg

1 tsp fine salt (to taste)

180g/6¾oz chickpea flour

195ml/6½fl oz dairy-free milk

1 yellow plantain

1 medium courgette

1 red onion

2 red peppers, deseeded

200g/7oz button mushrooms

The ose oji sauce

300g/10½oz smooth unsalted peanut butter

1 tbsp ground cayenne pepper

1 tsp ground nutmeg

½ tsp fine salt

Preheat the oven to 200°C/400°F (180°C/350°F fan). Soak the wooden skewers in water for 15 minutes.

Pulse the peanuts in a food processor for a couple of seconds, until lightly blended. Then shake them onto a large plate with the garlic powder, stock cube, spices and salt.

Put the chickpea flour and milk in a medium bowl and whisk together with a pinch of salt until you have a smooth, thick batter.

Top and tail the plantain, then score the skin down the length of it, trying not to cut through to the flesh. Repeat down the opposite length and remove the skin. Chop up the plantain, courgette, onion and red peppers into chunks and rounds, trying to keep the sizes broadly the same. Keep the mushrooms whole. Assemble the kebabs by gently pushing alternating vegetables along the skewers.

Using large spoonfuls, coat each kebab in the batter. Let any excess batter drip off into the bowl, then roll the kebabs across the plate of peanuts and spice mix.

Transfer them to an aluminium foil-lined tray and cook in the centre of the oven for 15–20 minutes, until the vegetables are tender.

For the ose oji, stir together the peanut butter, spices and salt in a saucepan and warm up over a medium-low heat.

Serve the kebabs hot, drizzled with the ose oji. Top with crushed roasted peanuts and a sprinkling of coriander, if you like, keeping any extra sauce on the side for dipping.

Àgbàdo àti Àgbọ̀n (Sweetcorn and Coconut)

Serves 2–3 | 20 minutes

Àgbàdo àti àgbọ̀n, 'fresh sweetcorn and coconut', is a delicious snack sometimes sold by Nigerian street hawkers. But this recipe takes that flavour combination a step further, by adding another level of texture through roasted peanuts, and drenching everything in lime juice and spicy-sweet seasoning. If you're using a fresh coconut, follow the instructions on how to split it on p.112.

30g/1oz fresh coconut flakes (you can buy these or follow the instructions on p.112 to make your own)

3 fresh corn-on-the-cobs

30g/1oz roasted unsalted peanuts

1 tbsp melted vegan butter (or roasted peanut oil)

2 limes (1 juiced, 1 to garnish)

½ red onion, finely chopped

small handful of coriander, finely chopped

1 garlic clove, minced

½ tsp fine salt

½ tsp chilli powder

½ tsp ground cumin

½ tsp freshly ground black pepper

1 tsp brown sugar

Heat your oven to 200°C/400°F (180°C/350°F fan) and scatter the fresh coconut flakes onto a greased oven tray. Place them in the oven for 10 minutes, stirring every 2–3 minutes, until nice and toasty. Then set aside.

Boil a large pot of salted water. Remove the husks from the corn-on-the-cobs, cut them in half widthways and add them to the pot. Boil for 5–7 minutes, until you notice the sweetcorn kernels saturating in colour. Drain.

Using a sharp knife, cut the corn kernels away from the cob and put them in a bowl with the roasted coconut and the peanuts. Toss well in the melted vegan butter (or oil) and lime juice, along with all of the other ingredients.

Serve fresh with extra wedges of lime for squeezing.

Jollof Arancini

Serves 4 (about 16 arancini) | 2 hours

To the delight of Nigerian foodies, leftover jollof rice (p.48) can be turned into wonderful arancini in this Afro-Italian fusion recipe – deep-fried rice balls, with a spiced crust and a sweet, caramelly filling. In this recipe, I've made the jollof a bit stickier than usual to allow for the arancini to take shape more easily, but if you are starting with leftover jollof, I would recommend binding the rice together with plenty of good quality, meltable vegan cheese and a 'flax egg' (flaxseed meal mixed with water). Serve the arancini on a bed of rocket to help give the illusion of a well-balanced meal, or splatter them with chilli sauce and enjoy fresh out the pan.

The jollof rice

2 medium plum tomatoes

2 red peppers

1 small Scotch bonnet

1 red onion (½ chopped, ½ sliced)

1½ tbsp vegetable oil

2 garlic cloves, crushed

½ tsp smoked paprika

½ tsp cayenne pepper

1½ tsp curry powder

1 tsp ground ginger

½ tsp ground turmeric

1 vegetable stock cube, crumbled

1 tsp fine salt

1 tsp freshly ground black pepper

1 tbsp tomato purée

200g/7oz long-grain rice

1½ tsp dried thyme

1 bay leaf

1 tbsp flaxseed meal

vegetable oil, for deep-frying

Roughly chop the tomatoes, red peppers and Scotch bonnet, then add them to a blender or food processor with the chopped ½ an onion and pulse until smooth. Set aside.

Heat the vegetable oil in a medium sauté pan or casserole dish over a medium heat. Add the sliced ½ an onion to the pan. Cook for 15 minutes until golden. Stir in the garlic and cook for 1 minute. Add the spices, stock cube, salt and pepper and cook for 1 minute more.

Squeeze in the tomato purée, then stir well. Add the blended tomato and pepper mixture. Bring to a simmer, then cover, leaving the lid slightly ajar, and cook for 20–25 minutes until you have a thick sauce, stirring occasionally to make sure it doesn't burn.

Meanwhile, parboil the rice. First, rinse it really well in a sieve until the water runs almost clear, then cover generously with boiling water in a saucepan. Bring to the boil, cover and simmer for no more than 5 minutes; it should still be really firm. Drain the rice and set aside.

When the sauce has had its time and thickened, stir in the parboiled rice, dried thyme and bay leaf and add 400ml/13½fl oz water. Stir well, bring to the boil, then reduce the heat to medium-low. Put on the lid, leaving it slightly ajar, and cook for 20–25 minutes, until the rice is al dente and the liquid has

The filling

2 very ripe (almost black) plantains, peeled

2 red peppers

1 red onion

2 tbsp vegetable oil

1 lime, zested and juiced

The coating

60g/2¼oz cornflour

110ml/3¾fl oz non-dairy milk (full-fat oat or soya is best)

75g/2¾oz panko breadcrumbs

To serve

handful of rocket leaves

vegan parmesan, grated

been absorbed. Leave the rice to cool completely; spreading it out on a tray speeds up the process.

Meanwhile, start the filling. Heat the oven to 230°C/450°F (210°C/410°F fan). Finely chop the plantains, red peppers and onion, then place them on a baking tray and sprinkle with a big pinch of salt. Drizzle the oil over them, toss well and roast for 25–30 minutes, stirring halfway. Empty them into a bowl and toss with the lime zest and juice. Set aside and turn the oven down to 180°C/350°F (160°C/325°F fan).

Combine the flaxseed meal with 2½ tablespoons of water and leave it to sit for 5 minutes. When the rice is completely cool, remove the bay leaf. Stir the flaxseed meal mixture (a flax egg) into the rice. Now stir in half of the roasted plantain, red pepper and onion filling mixture.

Set out three bowls for the coating; one each for the cornflour, the milk and the breadcrumbs. Wet your hands so the rice doesn't stick to your fingers. Roll handfuls to the size of golf balls, flatten, then place a small spoonful of the remaining roasted vegetable filling inside before rolling it back up into a ball. Dip each ball in the cornflour, then the milk, then finally the breadcrumbs. Set aside. Chill them in the fridge if you need to firm them up.

Half-fill a wide pan with vegetable oil and place over a high heat. Line a plate with kitchen paper. When the oil is hot, add 4 balls and fry until golden, turning halfway, then transfer to the lined plate. Repeat with the remaining balls.

Serve warm on a bed of rocket, topped with plenty of grated vegan parmesan. You could drizzle over some ata dindin (p.133), if you like.

Oun

tí o bá

gbìn

lo má

ká

What you plant is what you will pluck

Classic Àkàrà (Black-Eyed Bean Fritters)

Serves 6–8 | 45 minutes

Àkàrà goes by many names – accra, akla, acarajé, kosai and koosé to name a few – because it's enjoyed in so many countries across West Africa, as well as in Brazil. It's often served for breakfast with ogi (a fermented maize custard), sweet soft agege bread and fried plantain (p.99), and they're really set off by a good chilli sauce like ata dindin (pictured here, with recipe on p.133). It may be a labour of love to peel the beans, but it's well worth the effort; an easier alternative is black-eyed bean flour, but it's a little drier tasting.

400g/14oz dried black-eyed beans or bean flour

1 red pepper, finely chopped

1 red onion, finely chopped

1 Scotch bonnet (to taste), finely chopped

1 vegetable stock cube, crumbled

1 tsp ground ginger

½ tsp fine salt

½ tsp freshly ground black pepper

vegetable oil or sustainable red palm oil, for deep-frying

To serve

handful of fresh parsley, chopped

ata dindin (optional, p.133)

Soak the beans in warm water for 15 minutes to loosen the skins. Take one between your fingers and rub off the skin. If it doesn't come off, keep soaking and check again. Once the skins can be rubbed off easily, drain the beans and (skins still on) add a handful of them to a blender or food processor half-filled with water. Pulse briefly to break them up a little, then sieve. Tip the sieve full of beans and skins into a large bowl and cover with water. The skins should rise to the top; pour them off and discard, leaving the beans at the bottom of the bowl. Fill the bowl again, agitate the beans, and repeat until all the skins are off, picking the last few by hand. Repeat until you have removed all of the bean skins.

For the batter, tip the peeled beans (or bean flour) back into the blender or food processor with just a splash of water to help get it going, and pulse until smooth. If it's too liquid, it won't hold its shape when fried. Add all the other ingredients except the oil and pulse again. Half-fill a wide saucepan with oil and put it over a medium-high heat. Line a colander with kitchen paper.

Test the heat by dropping a small amount of batter into the oil; if it floats, it's ready. Fry spoonfuls of the batter at a time, without crowding the pan, turning carefully halfway through so they cook evenly. Once brown, transfer each fritter to the prepared colander. Garnish with the chopped parsley, then serve fresh, with a bowl of ata dindin on the side to dip, if you like.

Cheesy Kokoro

Serves 10 | 45 minutes

Kokoro is a crispy, golden and supremely crunchy street food made from cornmeal. It's predominantly sold along the roads of south-west Nigeria, particularly in Abeokuta. This version comes with vegan parmesan and fresh parsley and is ideal for those listless moments when you just don't know what to munch on – but you want it to be good. It's best enjoyed hot and dunked in fresh chilli sauce (p.124 or 133). Cue chef kissing fingertips!

340g/12oz coarse or granulated cornmeal

60g/2oz white garri

1 tbsp cane sugar (or granulated sugar)

4 garlic cloves, minced

1 tsp cayenne pepper

½ tsp ground ginger

½ tsp fine salt

½ tsp nutmeg

1 vegetable stock cube (preferably Maggi), crumbled

1 tbsp nutritional yeast

2 tbsp good quality vegan parmesan, finely grated

2 tbsp fresh parsley, finely chopped

vegetable oil or other flavourless oil, for deep-frying

Combine all the ingredients, apart from the oil, in a large bowl. Bring 500ml/1 pint water to the boil in a medium saucepan. Pour the mixture into the saucepan, stirring continuously as you do until a dough starts to form. Remove from the heat, tip back into the bowl, and knead until you have a smooth ball of dough.

Roll the dough into breadsticks about 1cm/½in thick and 15–20cm/6–8in long. The slimmer they are, the crunchier they'll be. If the dough sticks, lightly oil your hands.

Place some kitchen paper on a plate, ready. Half-fill a large, wide frying pan with vegetable oil and heat. Add the kokoro sticks and fry until golden and crisp, rolling over occasionally so that all sides cook evenly. Be careful to not crowd the frying pan.

Transfer the kokoro to the plate as soon as they're done and leave to cool for 10 minutes before serving.

Dodo
(Fried Plantain)

Serves 4 | 30 minutes

Plantain is an absolute Nigerian favourite, and dodo possibly its most popular incarnation, loved by everyone for its natural, caramelly sweetness. If you're looking for an easy recipe to get started with, dodo's the one. It's not only foolproof, but hugely versatile; pack it warm onto jollof (p.48), yellow rice (p.62) or coconut rice (p.75), have it as a side or starter, drizzle it with lime or submerge in hot ata dindin sauce (p.133).

3 ripe yellow plantains

3 tbsp coconut oil

½ red onion, thinly sliced

1 tsp crushed dried chillies

¼ tsp sea salt

handful of fresh parsley, chopped

Top and tail the plantains, then score the skin down the length of each, trying not to cut through to the flesh. Repeat down the opposite length and remove the skin. Slice the plantain flesh diagonally to create oval slices. Get a plate lined with kitchen paper ready.

Heat the coconut oil in a large frying pan over a medium heat. (Some people like to deepen the flavour of the coconut oil by frying a sliced onion in it before cooking the plantain. Remove the onion before the plantain goes in.)

When the oil's hot, spoon in small batches of the plantain and cook for 5 minutes on each side, until golden. Don't crowd the frying pan. Transfer cooked batches to the kitchen paper and repeat, adding a little more oil to the pan if needed.

Once all the plantain is cooked, put it in a large bowl along with the raw, sliced red onion, crushed chilli, sea salt and the chopped parsley, then gently toss together for serving. Add a pinch of cayenne pepper for some extra heat or a squeeze of lime for tang, if you like.

Moi Moi
(Steamed Bean Puddings)

Serves 4 | 1 hour 45 minutes, plus soaking time

Moi moi (or moin moin) is a trusty staple in Nigeria, often teamed with jollof (p.48), yellow rice (p.62), coconut rice (p.75) or dodo (p.99), or enjoyed for breakfast with ogi (a fermented maize custard). Traditionally, it's steamed wrapped in ewe eran leaves, which lends it a subtly sweet flavour. But for simplicity I like using cupcake moulds. This recipe fills 15–18 typical moulds, so you'll need two cupcake trays (and cases to go with them). If you can't get Nigerian honey beans, it's also really good made with black-eyed or drum beans.

400g/14oz dried Nigerian honey beans (oloyin)

2 red peppers, 1 roughly and 1 finely chopped

½ red onion, roughly chopped

1 Scotch bonnet (to taste), roughly chopped

1 vegetable stock cube, crumbled

1½ tsp ground nutmeg

1 tsp chilli powder

½ tsp smoked paprika

1 tsp fine salt

3 tbsp sustainable red palm oil

small bunch of coriander, finely chopped (optional), plus extra leaves to garnish

The method for peeling the beans is the same as for classic àkàrà (p.94). When the skins are off, rinse the beans one last time, and soak them for at least 4 hours or overnight.

Heat the oven to 180°C/350°F (160°C/325°F fan). Drain the beans, then add them to a blender or food processor with the roughly chopped red pepper, red onion, Scotch bonnet and 350ml/11¾fl oz water and blend to a smooth batter. Set aside.

Dissolve the stock cube in 1½ tablespoons of boiling water in a small bowl, with the spices and salt. Then stir in the oil. Whisk this mixture into the batter for 5 minutes, until fluffy. Fold the finely chopped red pepper (and coriander, if using) into the batter.

Line two cupcake trays with 15–18 cases. Pour the batter into them and place the trays into roasting tins, so that they fit inside easily. Half-fill the roasting tins with boiling water to create a water bath. Cover tightly with oiled aluminium foil and transfer to the oven.

Bake for 25–30 minutes, until a toothpick comes out clean. Let them rest for 10–15 minutes, then remove from their cases and serve with a scattering of coriander leaves.

Àkàrà Onion Rings

Serves 6 | 1 hour 30 minutes

This riff on classic àkàrà (p.94) borrows the black-eyed bean batter to make super-crisp, yet melt-in-your-mouth onion rings. The process of peeling the beans is exactly the same (and just as fiddly), but you can save yourself some time using bean flour instead, although it's a little drier on the tongue. Get the batter thick enough to really bring out that distinctive àkàrà flavour, and feel free to supplement or replace the red palm oil with vegetable oil when deep-frying.

150g/5oz plain flour

150g/5oz panko breadcrumbs

2 large red onions, cut into 1½cm/½in rings

sustainable red palm oil, for deep-frying

The batter

370g/13oz dried black-eyed beans or bean flour

1 medium red onion, finely diced

1 medium red pepper, finely diced

1 Scotch bonnet (to taste), deseeded and finely chopped

15g/½oz parsley, finely chopped

1 vegetable stock cube, crumbled

1 tsp freshly ground black pepper

1 tsp fine salt

To serve

handful of fresh parsley, chopped

½–1 tsp red pepper flakes, to taste

ata dindin (optional, p.133)

lemon wedges

First, make the batter. If you're using beans, follow the instructions on how to peel them on p.94. Tip the peeled beans or bean flour and 150ml/5fl oz water into a blender or food processor and pulse until thick and smooth, then pour the mixture into a medium-sized mixing bowl. Stir in all of the remaining batter ingredients.

Next, place the flour and breadcrumbs into two separate, shallow bowls. Dip one of the onion rings into the àkàrà batter, followed by the flour bowl, and then again in the batter. Use your hands to pack on as much of the batter mix as possible. Finally, dip it into the breadcrumbs and transfer it to a tray. Repeat the process for all the rings.

Half-fill a wide saucepan with red palm oil and place over a medium-high heat. Once the oil is hot (about 170°C/340°F if you have an oil thermometer), fry the onion rings in batches, for 4–5 minutes each until golden and crisp, turning halfway through. Use a slotted spoon to lift them from the oil and onto a tray lined with kitchen paper, then sprinkle each batch with a pinch of salt.

Serve warm, garnished with the parsley and red pepper flakes, a bowl of ata dindin to dip, if you like, and lemon wedges for squeezing.

Beetroot Flatbread

Makes 8-10 | 1 hour

Though flatbreads are not a staple Nigerian food, this colourful and aromatic remix of the humble Lebanese bread is made to be paired with my shawarma recipe (p.58) – but actually goes with just about everything. And it's surprisingly easy to do – not at all as laborious as 'making bread' sounds, yet coming with all the bragging rights. You can make your own beetroot juice too, by blending raw beetroots with a dash of water into a purée and straining through a cheesecloth.

400g/14oz plain flour, plus extra for dusting

2½ tsp hickory smoke powder (optional)

1½ tsp caster sugar

1½ tsp ground cumin

1 tsp baking powder

1 tsp garlic powder

1 tsp fine salt

1 tsp freshly ground black pepper

200ml/6¾fl oz beetroot juice

95ml/3¼fl oz extra virgin olive oil

Sieve all the dry ingredients into a large mixing bowl or stand mixer. Mix well with a wooden spoon (or, if using a stand mixer, use the dough hook), all the while adding the beetroot juice and 80ml/2¾fl oz of the olive oil in small increments, until the dough sticks together into one ball.

On a floured work surface, divide the dough into 8-10 balls, depending how large you'd like your flatbread. Dust the balls with flour, then press them down into patties, keeping them even and circular. Cover with a tea towel and leave to rest for 20 minutes.

Cut two 21cm/8¼in-square pieces of baking parchment. Place a dough patty onto one of the squares, then put the other square on top. With a rolling pin, roll the dough into a circle, keeping within the bounds of the parchment square and turning it through quarters as you go to maintain a circular shape. Remove onto a floured surface and repeat with the other patties.

Heat the remaining olive oil in a non-stick frying pan over a medium heat. Cook each flatbread for a couple of minutes on either side, until areas of the bread start to turn golden, retaining as much of the colourful brightness as possible. Turn down the heat if they are browning too fast.

Wrap the cooked flatbreads in a clean tea towel to keep them soft and warm while you work. Enjoy while warm and fresh.

Pekere
(Chilli Plantain Crisps)

Serves 6 | 50 minutes

These naturally gluten-free, ever-so-slightly-sweet crisps are made from unripe green plantains. Pekere is sold on almost every street corner in Nigeria, tightly wrapped in plastic and stacked in large elegant piles, or balanced on street vendors' headwraps, or both! My siblings and I used to fight like crazy over them, and crammed them into our suitcases when we went to school abroad for a taste of home. Not just a madly popular street-food snack, pekere gives some serious crunch when crushed over stews or salads.

3 green plantains

3 tbsp vegetable oil

2 tsp light brown sugar

1½ tsp flaky sea salt

1 tsp cayenne pepper

1 tsp smoked paprika

½ tsp chilli powder

Preheat your oven to 200°C/400°F (180°C/350°F fan). Line two large oven trays with baking parchment.

Top and tail the plantains. Draw a knife down the length of each, scoring the skin but trying not to cut through the flesh. Repeat down the opposite side and remove the skin. Slice them as thinly as you can to achieve a crispy, non-chewy finish – a mandolin comes in handy here.

In a large bowl, toss the plantain in the vegetable oil with the brown sugar, salt, cayenne pepper, smoked paprika and chilli powder, ensuring the pieces are fully coated.

Lay the slices out on the baking trays, making sure they're spaced out. Transfer to the oven to bake for 10 minutes, then turn the slices over and cook for a further 5-10 minutes, depending on the thickness of your slices, until crisp and golden.

Remove the crisps from the oven, and leave to cool. Repeat the cooking process with the remaining plantain.

Serve straight away, or let cool completely and store in an airtight container to snack on later. They stay crisp for 3-4 days.

Spicy Yam Bites

Makes 8-10 bites | 1 hour 20 minutes

Mashed yams, moulded into balls, rolled in spices and baked, are so good. That's why street-sellers do a roaring trade with them across Nigeria and Ghana. (To be honest, the Ghanaians are the absolute masters at cooking yam!) Perhaps it's the high starchiness of the yam, without being too sugary like a sweet potato, that makes it so delicious. I like filling mine with this tangy-sweet roasted pepper sauce, which my lovely friend, Emily, said was like a Spanish Romesco with a kick. You could also just use it as a dip for smaller bites with no filling, or make extra to enjoy later – with fresh bread or anything you can think of. If you have yam left over after making this recipe, roast it in plenty of vegan butter and serve with chilli sauce.

The filling

3 red peppers

2 garlic cloves

2 tbsp olive oil

1 small Scotch bonnet

100g/3½oz raw cashews

handful of fresh coriander

1 tbsp white wine vinegar

1 tbsp brown sugar

1 tsp fine salt

The yam

500g/1lb 2oz puna yam

170g/6oz vegan butter

1 tsp fine salt

Start with the filling. Preheat the oven to 200°C/400°F (180°C/350°F fan). Deseed and roughly chop the red peppers, peel the garlic, then place them both on an oven tray. Toss in the oil and roast for 30 minutes, stirring halfway. Blitz the roasted peppers and garlic with the rest of the filling ingredients in a blender or food processor until smooth. Set aside.

Prepare the yam by peeling and chopping it into 4cm/1½in chunks. Boil the chunks in salted water for 15-20 minutes until soft. Drain, then mash the yam with the butter and salt while it's still hot.

Mould the mash to the size of golf balls. The mixture can be crumbly so squeeze tightly. Supporting it with your hand, poke a deep hole in each ball and spoon some of the filling into its centre. Cover the hole and roll it into a ball again. Reheat the oven to 200°C/400°F (180°C/350°F fan) and lightly grease a baking tray.

Now, make the batter. Set out two bowls. Mix the oat milk (soya will do) and lemon juice in one and combine all dry ingredients, minus the cornmeal, in the other. Set aside 1 tablespoon of the dry ingredients for later, then stir in the cornmeal.

The batter

200ml/6¾fl oz full-fat oat milk

1 tbsp lemon juice

1 tbsp ground cloves

2 tsp smoked paprika

1½ tsp brown sugar

1½ tsp ground nutmeg

1½ tsp ground cinnamon

1 tbsp hickory smoke powder

1 tsp cayenne pepper

2 tsp fine salt

100g/3½oz yellow cornmeal

Lightly roll the yam balls in the dry ingredients, then the wet, then the dry again, before transferring to the baking tray. You can recoat the balls with any leftovers if you like. Bake them for 15–20 minutes until they firm up a bit. When ready, leave them to cool for 10 minutes.

Serve them warm, sprinkled with the tablespoon of reserved spices and with any extra filling as a dip. You could also try garnishing them with roughly chopped coriander and serving with some cooling coconut yoghurt – or have them plain with a bowl of red-hot chilli sauce on the side.

Aunty Keffi's Fresh Coconut Chips

Serves 2-3 | 55 minutes

My gorgeous Aunty Keffi is a walking treasure trove of information when it comes to making simple, healthy veggie snacks. Aunty's special touch to these deceptively simple coconut chips is the addition of turmeric and cumin, which adds warmth and somehow, for me, a sense of abundance. She also recommends rubbing them with suya spice (p.121), a traditional blend of peanuts and spices more commonly used on kebabs (p.84). Thank you, Aunty Keffi – and my younger cousins Rocco and Ini for being our miniature recipe testers!

1 fresh, mature coconut

½ tsp ground turmeric

⅓ tsp ground cumin

⅓ tsp paprika

⅓ tsp cayenne pepper

⅛ tsp (or a generous pinch) fine salt

⅛ tsp freshly ground black pepper

vegetable oil, for greasing

Preheat your oven to 200°C/400°F (180°C/350°F fan). To remove the juice from the coconut, look for the 'eyes' at the top, then carefully press in a screwdriver. One is always softer than the others. Turn it upside down over a glass to empty the liquid. (You can drink this now, or put it in the fridge to enjoy later.)

Lay your coconut on a baking tray and bake it in the oven for 20 minutes. Take it out, but leave the oven on. While the coconut's cooling, combine all the spices and seasonings in a medium bowl. Grease a baking tray with oil.

Place the coconut on a chopping board and carefully tap its centre with a hammer. Turn the coconut and keep hammering along a central line until it cracks, then prise it open with a butter knife until it breaks in half.

Using a firm spoon, scrape the flesh away from the shell, and put the shell aside for later. With a peeler, slice the flesh to create large, curvy chips. Toss the chips in the spice mix until coated, then tip them onto the greased oven tray. Pop them in the oven and roast for 15-20 minutes, stirring now and then, until golden.

Serve the chips fresh and hot in one of the emptied coconut shells.

Plantain Curls

Serves 4 | 30 minutes

Golden spiralling curls of plantain, sweetly fragrant and infused with smoked hickory, are a family favourite of ours. Whenever I make them, I feel obliged to send photos to my youngest sister who always says, 'I can taste these just by looking at them.' You don't have to deep-fry them, either: they work just as well barbecued, and will be a total revelation for the uninitiated at your next cook-out.

4 large green plantains

1 tbsp hickory smoke powder (or liquid smoke, brushed on)

2½ tsp onion powder

2 tsp ground ginger

1½ tsp light brown sugar

1½ tsp garlic powder

1 tsp ground nutmeg

1 tsp fine salt

1 tsp freshly ground black pepper

½ tsp ground cayenne pepper

8 wooden skewers

vegetable oil, for deep-frying

To serve

handful of fresh coriander, chopped

ata dindin (optional, p.133)

Top and tail the plantains, then score the skin down the length of each, trying not to cut through to the flesh. Repeat down the opposite length and remove the skin. Slice the plantains in half across widthways.

Mix together all the spices and seasonings in a bowl, tip them onto a plate and set aside.

Skewer the centre of each plantain half, from top to bottom. Now spiralise the plantains with a small sharp knife. Starting at one end, slice down to the skewer and rotate the plantain while moving the knife steadily against the skewer towards the other end. Repeat with each plantain. Thin plantains will break, but you can cut them into rounds instead and skewer them for a similar effect.

Tease the spirals a little apart along the skewers, so there's space between the curls. Roll each plantain in the spice mix.

(If you're barbecueing, now's the time to put them on the grill; cook for 30 minutes, turning regularly until all sides are golden.)

Heat enough vegetable oil to go over halfway up the plantains in a wide frying pan over a medium-high heat. When hot, fry the plantains in batches for 3–5 minutes, turning once, and remove to a tray lined with kitchen paper. Sprinkle with any remaining spices and put on a serving plate. Garnish with the fresh coriander and enjoy with ata dindin, if you like.

Gúgúrú àti Ẹ̀pà
(Spicy Popcorn and Peanuts)

Serves 8–10 | 20 minutes

As a kid, I spent a fair amount of time shuttling along the Lagos–Ibadan expressway, a journey that somehow fluctuated between two and eight hours. This was when I ate all my favourite snacks, including spicy popcorn (gúgúrú) and dry-roasted peanuts (ẹ̀pà), which are sold in Lagos on the street, neatly wrapped in cones of newspaper. I love putting the last two together as one. So, here's a crunchy snack with a bit of a kick that's easy to make and even more addictive to eat.

5 tbsp vegetable oil

200g/7oz popcorn kernels

5 tbsp caster sugar

285g/10oz unsalted dry-roasted peanuts

1 tsp fine salt

½ tsp cayenne pepper

Heat the vegetable oil over a high heat in a large saucepan that has a lid. Check the oil is ready by adding a couple of popcorn kernels and seeing if they pop. Then pour in the rest of the kernels and the sugar, give everything a quick stir, and put on the lid.

Let the kernels pop, but shake the pan well and regularly to stop them burning.

Once the popping comes to an end, pour the popcorn into a large bowl and mix with the dry-roasted peanuts, salt and cayenne pepper. Discard any burnt or un-popped pieces.

Serve it in a large bowl or, for the full street-food experience, twirl some newspaper into cones and serve each portion in them, Lagos style.

Battered Okra with Avocado and Coriander Dip

Serves 6–8 | 40 minutes

In Nigeria, okra is most often used for okro soup, a delicacy also called 'draw soup' because of its sticky, viscous texture as you draw it from the bowl. I like to batter my okra in heavily spiced cornmeal, deep-fry it and serve it with this zingy avocado dip – a guaranteed crowd-pleaser.

200ml/6¾fl oz full-fat, dairy-free milk

1 tsp lemon juice

1 tsp garlic powder or granules

1 tbsp fresh thyme, finely chopped

1 tsp ground cumin

½ tsp cayenne pepper

½ tsp ground cinnamon

½ tsp onion powder or granules

1 tsp fine salt

½ tsp freshly ground black pepper

150g/5oz plain flour

75g/2¾oz yellow cornmeal

300g/10½oz fresh okra, tops cut off

vegetable oil, for deep-frying

The dip

1 medium avocado

100g/3½oz dairy-free yoghurt

2 tbsp olive oil

50g/2oz fresh coriander, chopped

2 garlic cloves

½ tsp fine salt

½ tsp freshly ground black pepper

1 lime, zested and juiced

Combine the milk and lemon juice in a shallow bowl, then leave to sit for 5 minutes.

Mix the spices and seasonings in a medium bowl. Take a heaped teaspoon of the mix and keep aside for later. Add half of the flour and all of the yellow cornmeal to the bowl. Put the rest of the flour, along with a pinch of salt and pepper, into another bowl.

Slice the okra in half lengthways or, if large, in quarters lengthways. Dip an okra in the bowl of flour, salt and pepper, to coat. Next, dip it in the milk and lemon mixture. Finally, roll it in the bowl with the flour, cornmeal and spices. Make sure you pack this onto the okra to get a nice, thick coat. Repeat with all of the okra.

Half-fill a wide frying pan with vegetable oil and place over a high heat, then line a plate with some kitchen paper. When the oil's hot, fry the okra in small batches, so as not to overcrowd the pan, for 4–5 minutes each until golden, turning halfway. Remove to the lined plate, repeat with the rest, then leave to cool while you make the dip.

Peel and destone the avocado, then put all of the dip ingredients into a blender or food processor, keeping back a little coriander to garnish at the end. Blitz, then scoop into a small bowl.

Sprinkle the reserved teaspoon of spices across the okra, garnish with coriander and serve fresh.

Suya-Roasted Chickpeas

Serves 3 | 45 minutes

This is a great snack on its own, to wolf down or nibble on throughout the day – but equally good scattered across fresh green salads, or as a spicy crouton-like topping for a creamy soup. There's plenty of room for experimentation, too; you may want to adjust the saltiness and heat of the suya spice mix (a blend of peanuts and spices more commonly used for kebabs, see p.84), or make it less punchy by increasing the proportion of peanuts. A shorter cooking time makes for a chewier, 'meatier' finish, while longer on a lower heat gives you a really hard crunch.

400g/14oz can chickpeas

1½ tbsp vegetable oil

½ tsp fine salt (to taste)

The suya spice mix

100g/3½oz roasted unsalted peanuts

¾ tsp garlic powder

½ vegetable stock cube, crumbled

1 tsp cayenne pepper (to taste)

1 tsp paprika

1 tsp ground ginger

¼ tsp ground cloves

¼ tsp allspice

¼ tsp ground nutmeg

Preheat the oven to 180°C/350°F (160°C/325°F fan) and line an oven tray with baking parchment. Rinse and drain the chickpeas, then blot dry with a tea towel to remove any excess moisture.

When preparing the suya spice mix, blitz the peanuts in a food processor first, being careful not to turn them into peanut butter. Turn them out onto a clean tea towel, roll up, twist and squeeze to release as much oil as possible. Then loosen them up with your fingers and mix together with all of the spices in a large bowl. If you like, you can pass the spice mix through a sieve for a finer texture, but I like to leave some slightly larger chunks of peanut.

Tip the chickpeas and vegetable oil into the suya spice mix. Toss until the chickpeas have a thick and even coating.

Empty the chickpeas onto the oven tray and roast for 30 minutes, stirring at 5–10 minute intervals.

Remove from the oven and leave to cool completely before serving. Sprinkle with the salt, to taste; you can also add some chilli flakes for extra heat, if you like. Store the chickpeas in an airtight container for a few days and use as a crunchy topping on salads, soups and stews.

DIPS & SAUCES

Kwaku's Famous (Very) Hot Sauce

Makes 2 standard jars | 50 minutes

Kwaku is my grandfather's utterly beloved family cook in Nigeria. He has been around for as long as I can remember and is known across Ibadan (my home city) for his wide smile and killer chilli sauce. We stir this into stews or soups for some sobering heat, or shake onto plantain curls (p.115), jollof arancini (p.88), or àkàrà (p.94) for a sublime fiery treat, but this miraculous sauce goes with almost everything. Feel free to swap out a few chillies for red peppers for less heat; it's seriously hot!

20 Scotch bonnets or habanero chillies

1 medium red onion, roughly diced

75g/3oz fresh ginger, peeled and finely chopped

4 garlic cloves, roughly chopped

2 lemons, zested and juiced

100ml/3½fl oz extra virgin olive oil

1 tsp ground cumin

1 tsp smoked paprika

1 tsp fine salt

Always use gloves when preparing the chillies. Deseed and roughly chop the Scotch bonnets (or habanero chillies). Add all ingredients to a food processor and pulse for a couple of seconds at a time, until everything is fairly finely chopped, but with a few chunks. You don't want a smooth paste.

Heat a medium-sized saucepan over a medium-high heat. Pour in the mixture and bring it to a vigorous simmer. Reduce the heat to a gentle simmer and leave for 30 minutes, keeping an eye on it and stirring every now and then to stop it catching on the bottom of the pan. You may want to open the windows, as the air gets pretty intense!

This sauce is quite thick, but you can add a couple of tablespoons of lemon juice or water if you like it thinner. Let it cool and enjoy as is, or store it in an airtight container or sterilised jars in the fridge.

Smoky Cashew and Beetroot Dip

Serves 6 | 1 hour 10 minutes, plus soaking time

Some of my fondest childhood memories are of our family cashew farm in Oyo state, where we harvested and dried the nuts in the blasting sun; visited our three monkeys Jo, Jojo and Joanna; and canoed over catfish ponds. The combination of cashew and tofu in this dip creates an exceptionally velvety texture, complemented by its head-turning bright pink colour, courtesy of the roasted beetroot. Its rich earthiness also acts as the perfect counterpart to the tangy lemon and the smoked hickory. With this dip in the frame, you won't want humous on your grazing tables for the foreseeable future!

4 small beetroots (about 450g/1lb)

3 large garlic cloves, unpeeled

4 tbsp extra virgin olive oil, plus extra for drizzling

3 tbsp lemon juice

150g/5oz raw unsalted cashews, soaked for 6 hours or overnight

100g/3½oz medium-firm tofu

2 tsp hickory smoke powder (or liquid smoke)

1 tsp fine salt

½ tsp freshly ground black pepper

2 spring onions, finely sliced diagonally

Serving suggestions

crudités, such as sliced raw carrot, cucumber, pepper, chicory or radishes

flatbread

Heat the oven to 200°C/400°F (180°C/350°F fan). Lay a sheet of aluminium foil on your worktop and put the beetroot and garlic cloves on top. Drizzle 1 tablespoon of the olive oil over them, sprinkle with salt and wrap up tightly to seal. Place the foil wrap on a baking tray and roast it in the oven for 1 hour, or until tender. Leave to cool, then peel and roughly chop the beetroot and remove the skin from the garlic cloves.

Tip the roasted beetroot and garlic into a blender or food processor with the lemon juice and remaining 3 tablespoons of olive oil and blitz until smooth. Drain the soaking cashews and add them to the blender or food processor, along with the tofu, hickory smoke powder (or liquid smoke), salt and pepper. Blend until completely smooth.

Spoon the dip into a bowl, top with the sliced spring onions, a drizzle of olive oil and some cracked black pepper, then serve fresh with crudités or sliced flatbread.

If you're keeping the dip for later use, it will thicken in the fridge. Add a little water to loosen it up.

Èmí

tí kò jata,

èmí

yẹpẹrẹ

ni

The soul that does not eat pepper
is a powerless soul

Ata Dindin (Chilli Sauce)

Makes 650ml/1¼ pints | 1 hour 30 minutes

This sauce marries two things I really love: a rich tomato-and-pepper base and a lot of heat. You can shake it over almost anything, thanks to its inherent ability to energise and transform whatever's on your plate. Feel free to experiment with the number of chillies you use to hit your ideal level of heat. In Yorùbá, ata dindin means 'fried pepper', and is cooked down to be much thicker than its cousin, ọbẹ ata (p.32), pepper stew.

30 bird's eye chillies

3 red peppers, diced

3 medium tomatoes, diced

2 tbsp tomato purée

1 red onion, finely diced

1 Scotch bonnet or habanero pepper, finely chopped

2 Maggi seasoning cubes (or other stock cubes)

2 tsp curry powder

1–2 tsp fine salt (to taste)

80ml/2¾fl oz vegetable oil

Wear gloves to deseed and destem the chillies. Place all the ingredients apart from the oil in a blender or food processor and blitz for about 2 minutes, or until completely smooth.

Heat the vegetable oil in a wide pot over a medium-high heat. Slowly pour in the pepper sauce mixture, bring to a gentle simmer, then cover the pot and reduce the heat.

Leave to cook for 1 hour, stirring at intervals. You may want to open the windows and get a good breeze going, as it gets pretty fierce.

Let the sauce cool and serve straight away or store in an airtight container in the fridge for up to a week.

SWEET TREATS

Hibiscus and Mint Chocolate Bark

Serves 6-8 | 20 minutes, plus chilling time

The exuberant appearance of this chocolate bark makes it a striking homemade gift or party snack. It's a little eccentric maybe, but I like to cover a cake with it, wrapped securely with jute string in a neat bow. The beautiful nutty aroma you'll notice as you make this comes from the cocoa butter (also known as white chocolate butter), one of the main ingredients of chocolate bars. Most of those have powdered milk and cocoa added, but this fruit-spotted recipe gets its creaminess from smooth cashew butter. To make professional-looking chocs instead, try using silicone baking moulds.

180g/6¾oz cocoa butter

4 tbsp extra virgin coconut oil

130g/4½oz icing sugar

2½ tbsp cashew butter (or almond butter) at room temperature

1½ tsp hibiscus powder

½ tsp vanilla powder (failing that, 2-3 drops vanilla extract)

½ tsp peppermint extract

¼ tsp fine salt

2 tsp dried hibiscus petals

handful of fresh mint leaves, larger leaves torn

handful of blueberries

handful of raspberries

handful of chopped pistachios

Tip the cocoa butter and coconut oil into a heatproof bowl. Fill a saucepan with a few centimetres (an inch or two) of water and bring to a simmer over a medium heat. Once simmering, place the bowl over the pan so that it fits snuggly but doesn't touch the water (a bain-marie), turn the heat down as low as possible and melt the cocoa butter and coconut oil, stirring regularly. Remove the bowl and leave to cool a little.

Place the icing sugar, cashew butter, hibiscus and vanilla powders, peppermint extract, salt and the melted cocoa butter and coconut oil into a blender or food processor and pulse until smooth.

Line a 20×30cm/8×12in lipped tray with baking parchment. Pour the blended chocolate mixture onto the tray and spread out until it's just under 1cm/½in thick. If it's too deep, some of your toppings may disappear into the chocolate.

Scatter over the hibiscus petals, mint leaves, blueberries, raspberries and pistachios, then put the tray in the fridge. Leave for 45 minutes-1 hour, until solid.

Remove from the fridge, crack the bark into pieces with the tip of a knife, and serve. It melts quite quickly so only take it out when you're ready to serve.

Nutty Plantain Brownies

Makes 12 | 1 hour, plus cooling time

These brownies are everything good brownies should be: decadent, moist, fudgy, and absolutely delicious to sink your teeth into. Most people think I'm joking when I say there's plantain in them, but this ingredient is actually the key to the lushness and makes the flavour all the more caramelly. The selection of nuts balances the sweet softness with a satisfying crunch for the ultimate rich treat – but you can get endlessly creative and load them up with your favourite goodies.

150g/5oz coconut oil, melted, plus extra for greasing

100g/3½oz cocoa powder, sieved, plus 2 tbsp for dusting

2 ripe yellow plantains (the skins will be splotchy black), peeled

125ml/4¼fl oz full-fat oat milk

1 tsp vanilla extract

150g/5oz plain flour, sieved

200g/7oz caster sugar

1½ tsp baking powder

¼ tsp fine salt

125g/4½oz hazelnuts, roughly chopped

125g/4½oz cashews, roughly chopped

150g/5oz vegan dark chocolate, chopped into small chunks

140g/4¾oz smooth peanut butter

Heat your oven to 180°C/350°F (160°C/325°F fan). Use a small amount of coconut oil to grease and line a 20cm/8in-square tin with baking parchment, then grease the parchment. Sprinkle the tin with the 2 tablespoons of cocoa powder, shaking and tapping it to make sure it's spread evenly. Set aside.

Tip the plantains, 150g/5oz coconut oil, the oat milk and vanilla extract into a blender or food processor and blitz until smooth, then pour into a medium bowl.

Sieve the flour, 100g/3½oz cocoa powder, sugar, baking powder and salt into a separate bowl, and tip into the wet mixture, combining well into a batter. Once smooth, stir in the nuts and chocolate, reserving a small handful of each for the topping. Pour the batter into your prepared tin and spread the mixture out evenly using the back of a spoon.

Drop the peanut butter in nine, roughly equal dollops across the tin and use a knife to marble it lightly into the batter, without mixing it too much. Scatter the reserved hazelnuts, cashews and chocolate chunks over the top, gently pushing them into the mixture.

Bake in the centre of the oven for 30–45 minutes, checking the brownies after 30 minutes, until the mixture is set but with a definite wobble in the centre. Leave in the tin to cool completely, then slice into 12 equal pieces for serving.

Cinnamon Puff-Puff

Makes about 40 | 35 minutes, plus rising time

Somewhere between bread rolls and miniature doughnuts, these fluffy bites of deep-fried gold are satisfyingly firm on the outside and as light as air within. Hugely popular in Nigeria, puff-puff are often the star feature of a plate of 'small chops' (finger food) at weddings and birthdays. Traditionally, they can be a savoury side or even a breakfast filler, but I love dredging them through a sugar-and-cinnamon coating, which turns them into an irresistible dessert or indulgent snack.

100g/3½oz golden caster sugar

2½ tsp active dry yeast

450g/1lb plain flour

2 tsp ground cinnamon

1 tsp ground nutmeg

1 tsp ground cardamom

1½ tsp fine salt

vegetable oil, for deep-frying

The coating

5 tbsp golden caster sugar

2 tsp ground cinnamon

1 tsp ground nutmeg

Put the sugar and yeast in a large bowl and add 450ml/3/4 pint warm water and let it sit for 5 minutes. Then sieve in the flour, cinnamon, nutmeg, cardamom and salt and whisk together until completely smooth. Cover with a clean tea towel and leave for around 1½ hours, or until the dough has doubled in size.

Meanwhile, combine the coating ingredients in a shallow bowl or on a plate and set aside. Place a large colander next to the stove, lined with kitchen paper.

When the dough is ready, half-fill a large pan with vegetable oil and warm over a high heat. Carefully drop a heaped table-spoon of dough into the hot oil; if it's hot enough (about 180°C/350°F if you have an oil thermometer), the dough should float. Continue dropping spoonfuls, but don't crowd the pan. Fry for around 2 minutes on either side, until they're deep brown all over.

Remove from the oil using a slotted spoon and transfer to the colander. Repeat for the rest of the batter.

While the puff-puff are still warm, roll them in the coating mix-ture (or have them plain with savouries), and serve immediately.

Avocado and Cocoa Raw Truffles

12–15 truffles | 1 hour 15 minutes

This is the kind of recipe made for those who say, 'I can't cook anything.' There's no cooking (just melting), and no elaborate ingredients or preparation. Short of munching on straight-up chocolate, these quick and guilt-free treats are pretty hard to beat. And I should know; I came up with this to satisfy a craving when I only had cocoa to hand, as well as mounds of the humongous avocados that grow in abundance in Nigeria. Try rolling the truffles in roasted hazelnuts or cocoa nibs, or putting a teaspoon of creamy peanut butter in the middle. The options are limitless!

150g/5oz vegan dark chocolate chips or finely chopped chocolate

1 medium avocado

1½ tbsp maple syrup

¼ tsp sea salt

½ tsp vanilla extract

3 tbsp roasted hazelnuts, finely chopped

3 tbsp cocoa powder

Put the chocolate in a heatproof bowl. Fill a saucepan with a few centimetres (an inch or two) of water and bring to a simmer over a medium heat. Once simmering, place the bowl over the pan so that it fits snuggly but doesn't touch the water (a bain-marie), turn the heat down as low as possible and melt the chocolate, stirring regularly.

Destone the avocado and scoop the flesh into a blender or food processor, along with the melted chocolate, maple syrup, salt and vanilla extract. Blend until smooth.

Scrape the mixture into a bowl and fold in the chopped hazelnuts. Cover and place in the fridge for 1 hour – this will make rolling the truffles easier.

Work spoonfuls of the mixture into walnut-sized balls, then roll in the cocoa powder to coat. Lay out on a plate to serve, or store in the fridge for up to a week to enjoy later.

Hibiscus and Coconut Nice-Cream

Serves 4 | 1 hour, plus freezing time

Despite appearances, this is a pretty effortless ice cream to make, with or without a machine. It's light and creamy, with silky coconut and tart hibiscus – a fruity flavour often compared with cranberry or pomegranate – and its fresh, pastel pink colour is just pure summer happiness in a bowl (or a coconut, as served here!). The vodka isn't for a secret kick; it's an optional extra that helps to keep the ice cream softer when frozen.

2 × 400ml/13½fl oz cans coconut cream

2 tbsp tapioca flour or cornflour

20g/¾oz dried hibiscus petals (or 1 tsp hibiscus powder)

2 tbsp maple syrup

2½ tbsp coconut oil

2½ tsp vodka (optional)

1 tsp vanilla or coconut extract

½ tsp fine salt

Garnish suggestions

2 tbsp dried hibiscus petals or hibiscus powder

2 tbsp desiccated coconut or toasted coconut flakes

Mix the coconut cream and tapioca flour (or cornflour) in a medium saucepan and bring it to a simmer over a medium-high heat, stirring frequently. Add the hibiscus petals (or powder), remove from the heat and leave to sit for 45 minutes.

If you're using petals, set a sieve over a bowl and strain the mixture to remove them. Press the petals into the sieve with the back of a spoon to squeeze all the mixture out before discarding.

Pour the mixture into a blender or food processor and add the rest of the ingredients, then pulse until well mixed and fluffy.

Chill the mixture in the fridge for 10 minutes, then churn in an ice-cream machine, if you have one, following the manufacturer's instructions. Alternatively, pour into a freezer-proof container, and place in the freezer for 3 hours. Remove and give it a really good stir before returning it to the freezer for another 2 hours. Remove, stir vigorously again, and repeat until you reach your desired creamy texture.

If garnishing with dried hibiscus petals, tip them into a pestle and mortar and crush.

Serve scoops of the ice cream topped with a sprinkling of coconut and a dusting of the hibiscus powder or petals.

Òjò tó
rọ̀ sí ewúro,
náà ló
rọ̀ sí ìrèké

The same rain that fell on the bitter leaf
fell on the sugarcane

Chin Chin Mango Cheesecake

Serves 10 | 1 hour, plus soaking and chilling time

This cheesecake is a concentrated dose of tropicality, thanks to its velvety-smooth mango and aromatic coconut filling. But that's not all. Its base of chin chin (crispy pieces of deep-fried dough, so-called because of the sound they make, like 'munch munch') is so addictive that I strongly recommend you cook an extra batch just for snacking – and to save your cheesecake crust from nibbles. Chin chin comes in all manner of shapes, from chunks to snakes to curls. Let your creativity run riot, as long as the chin chin is small enough to cook through. The same goes for the toppings; I never do the same twice, but I suggest some favourites in the recipe. You can also knock up this winning dessert in no time using shop-bought chin chin.

The chin chin

400ml/13½fl oz can coconut milk, chilled

4 tsp coconut oil, melted

370g/13oz plain flour

140g/4¾oz granulated sugar

⅛ tsp fine salt

1 tsp ground nutmeg

1 tsp ground cloves

1 tsp cinnamon

vegetable oil, for deep-frying

The cheesecake base

2 tbsp agave or maple syrup

100ml/3½fl oz coconut oil

To make the chin chin, start by scooping out 160g/5½oz of the solid part of the coconut milk (you can use the liquids for something else). Mix it with the coconut oil in one bowl, and mix together the dry ingredients in a separate bowl. Then combine both and knead into a dough.

Dust your work surface with flour. Break off 80g/3oz of the dough, and roll it into several long rolls, around 5mm/¼in thick, then chop into ½cm/¼in blocks. Roughly chop the rest of the dough – it doesn't need to be perfect as it will be crumbled for the cheesecake base.

Half-fill a large frying pan with vegetable oil and place over a high heat. Line a tray with kitchen paper. Once the oil is hot, deep-fry the finely cut dough pieces until golden, turning halfway, and transfer to the tray. Continue with the remaining 'rough' dough, frying in batches. Transfer this to the lined tray too to drain, but keep the two sets separate. Don't worry if the larger chunks break up a little when frying.

The cheesecake filling

500g/1lb 2oz frozen mango flesh

400ml/13½fl oz can coconut cream

400g/14oz cashews, soaked overnight

1 lemon, zested and juiced

2½ tbsp cocoa butter, melted

1 tsp vanilla extract

2 tsp ground turmeric

7 dates, pitted

1 tbsp agave or maple syrup

The toppings

handful of fresh raspberries

handful of fresh blueberries

For the base, put the rough batch in a food processor with the syrup and coconut oil. Season with a pinch of salt. Blitz until the mixture becomes crumbly. Line the base and sides of an 18cm/7in springform baking tin with baking parchment, then press the blitzed chin chin mixture into the bottom of it. Put it in the fridge to chill while you make the filling.

Blend all the filling ingredients (minus the syrup) in a blender or food processor until thick and creamy. Add the agave (or maple) syrup and taste, adding more sweetness if needed. Scoop the filling onto the cheesecake base, gently hitting the tin to help it flatten and release air bubbles.

Now for the toppings. Scatter the reserved (finely made) chin chin and the fresh berries on top of the filling, in a crescent moon shape, hugging the top corners of the cheesecake. My favourite extra toppings include crushed and dried hibiscus petals, fresh strawberries, lemon zest and quartered lemon slices. Whatever you include, try to keep all the garnishes within the crescent shape.

Place in the freezer to set for 4 hours, then transfer to the fridge for 1 hour before serving. Cut with a warm and clean knife for a smooth slice.

Spirulina and Coconut Energy Bites

Makes 12 | 25 minutes

Packed with protein and energy, these nutty blue-toned treats are the perfect afternoon pick-me-up. Not only are they quick and easy to make, all the ingredients store very well, so I find them a great option to make on Sundays to keep for the week ahead. Spirulina is no modern-day dietary fad; since at least the 9th century, the inhabitants of the Kanem Empire in Chad, which borders Nigeria, dried spirulina into edible cakes. They're still made and are now called dihé.

125g/4½oz desiccated coconut

75g/2¾oz almond flour (or ground almonds)

3 tbsp smooth almond butter

120g/4¼oz maple or agave syrup

1 tsp spirulina powder

pinch of fine salt

½ tsp coconut extract

½ tsp vanilla extract

85g/3oz pistachios, finely chopped

15g/½oz freeze-dried raspberries, finely chopped if whole

Combine 80g/3oz of the desiccated coconut with the almond flour, almond butter, maple (or agave) syrup, spirulina powder, salt and the coconut and vanilla extracts in a medium mixing bowl and stir until firm and malleable.

Stir in the chopped pistachios and freeze-dried raspberries.

Roll portions of the mixture almost to the size of golf balls, then coat in the remaining desiccated coconut.

They can be eaten there and then or stored in the fridge for about a week.

Mango Nice-Cream

Serves 6–8 | 30 minutes, plus chilling and freezing time

Full-on intense mango flavour. That's what hits you most about this recipe – and as you can make it with or without a churner, anyone can give it a go. Few things quite hit the spot like this ice cream shared with friends on a summer's day. Then again, no one could blame you for just stashing it in the freezer for whenever sweet cravings strike.

400ml/13½fl oz can full-fat coconut milk, chilled overnight in the fridge

220g/7¾oz condensed coconut milk, chilled overnight in the fridge

400g/14oz can Alphonso mango pulp

2½ tsp vodka (optional, to help keep the mixture smooth)

1 tbsp maple syrup (optional)

½ tsp fine salt

Serving suggestions (per person)

1 tsp desiccated coconut

1 tsp lime zest

1 tsp crushed pistachios

Open the tin of full-fat coconut milk and scoop the white solids into a bowl, leaving the transparent liquid (which you can use in smoothies, coffee or curries). Using a hand-held electric whisk, beat the coconut solids until fluffy.

Pour the condensed coconut milk into a large mixing bowl, and whisk for 2–5 minutes, until pale and creamy. Add the fluffy coconut solids to this bowl and whisk together for a further 2 minutes.

Tip in the mango pulp in small increments, while whisking, followed individually by the vodka, maple syrup (if you'd like your ice cream to be sweeter) and salt, whisking between each addition. If you have one, churn the mixture in an ice-cream machine following the manufacturer's instructions.

Otherwise, pour the mixture into a freezer-proof container and place in the freezer for 3 hours. After this time, remove and give it a really good stir before returning it to the freezer for another 2 hours. Remove, stir vigorously, and repeat until you reach your desired creamy texture. Before serving, let the ice cream thaw for 20 minutes so that it's scoopable.

Fluffy Coconut Layer Cake

Serves 10–12 | 1 hour 10 minutes

As soon as I was old enough to be left in the kitchen, I became the designated birthday-cake maker. And among cakes, if I had a speciality, this one would be it. I love its modest sweetness, the combination of soft sponge and crunchy flakes, and the tartness of lemon in the coconut frosting. It's really satisfying to chuck heaps of roasted coconut onto the cake, then step back to admire how quickly it takes shape as a messy three-layer masterpiece.

The cake

500ml/1 pint coconut milk (bottle or carton)

255g/9oz vegan butter, melted

2½ tsp apple cider vinegar

2 tsp vanilla extract

1 tbsp coconut extract

2 lemons, zested

525g/1lb 2½oz granulated sugar

460g/1lb ¼oz plain flour

3 tbsp cornflour

1½ tbsp baking powder

½ tsp fine salt

The frosting and topping

270g/9½oz unsalted vegan butter, softened

40ml/1¼fl oz coconut cream

1 lemon, juiced and zested

1 tbsp coconut extract

½ tsp vanilla extract

500g/1lb 2oz icing sugar

¼ tsp fine salt

125g/4½oz coconut flakes, toasted

Preheat your oven to 180°C/350°F (160°C/325°F fan). Grease three 20cm/8in cake tins and line the bases with baking parchment.

Combine all the wet cake ingredients and the lemon zest in a bowl and whisk well. Sieve the dry ingredients into a separate bowl and add them bit by bit to the wet ingredients, whisking until completely smooth. Divide the mixture between the three cake tins and bake for 30–40 minutes, until a skewer comes out clean. Leave to cool completely before removing from the tin.

While the cake is baking, make the frosting. Using a hand-held electric whisk, beat the soft butter with all the wet ingredients and the lemon zest in a large bowl for 3–5 minutes, until light and fluffy. In another bowl, sieve the icing sugar and add the salt. Whisk this into the wet ingredients in small increments until smooth. Chill in the fridge until firm enough to use.

Once the cake has cooled, level the layers with a levelling tool or long knife if you need to. Stack the layers, sandwiching the frosting between them. Pop the cake in the fridge if you need to firm it up.

Spread the remaining frosting across the outside of the cake. Lastly, press the coconut flakes all over the surface. Chill again to firm up, if needed, and serve. Store in the fridge.

DRINKS

The Nigerian Chapman

1 large pitcher | 10 minutes

A Chapman is a fizzy, red, non-alcoholic drink, slightly reminiscent of an English Pimm's, with a signature fruity lightness that has given it widespread popularity across Nigeria. Originating in the upmarket Ikoyi Club of Lagos, it's thought to be named after a British expat who asked the Nigerian bartender to fix him something refreshing. It's certainly that, and best enjoyed ice cold, tipped into a beer glass, poolside, next to a burning hot plate of suya kebabs (p.84). In Nigeria, the blackcurrant drink used is usually Ribena.

140ml/4¾fl oz grenadine syrup

300ml/10fl oz Fanta (or other fizzy orange)

300ml/10fl oz Sprite (or other lemonade)

75ml/2½fl oz blackcurrant drink (diluted, not concentrate)

1 tbsp Angostura bitters

3 tbsp undiluted zobo (optional, see p.166)

1 lemon, sliced

½ orange, sliced

½ cucumber, sliced into rounds or ribbons

handful of mint sprigs

In a large jug, combine the grenadine syrup, fizzy orange, lemonade, blackcurrant drink, Angostura bitters and zobo (if using). Add the lemon, orange and cucumber slices and the mint, and stir. Put the jug into the fridge to chill.

Serve over ice in a highball or beer glass garnished with a sprig of mint and decorate the rim with slices of cucumber or lemon. For next-level rim adornment, weave a long, thick shaving of cucumber over itself and skewer it with a toothpick as you go, before balancing the whole thing on the edge of the glass.

Moringa
Moon Milk

Makes 1 mug | 10 minutes

The moringa tree grows in Nigeria and across the tropics, and its leaves are an amazing source of vitamins, minerals and protein. They're dried for tea and powdered for food, and luckily you can find the powder in most good health food shops. Moringa's bittersweet, earthy taste works like a dream in smoothies, breakfast bowls, soups and even desserts (try it instead of spirulina to make energy balls, p.152). But I love it most in warm, spiced tiger nut milk before bedtime; it's so creamy and comforting, I find sleep is never very far away.

1 tsp agave or maple syrup (or 1 Medjool date, pitted)

240ml/8¼fl oz tiger nut milk (or your favourite dairy-free milk)

1 tsp extra virgin coconut oil

½ tsp moringa powder

¼ tsp ground cinnamon

⅛ tsp ground nutmeg

⅛ tsp ground cardamom

pinch of fine salt

Put all of the ingredients into a small saucepan. (If using the Medjool date instead of syrup, you'll need to tip all of the ingredients into a blender or food processor and blitz until you have a completely smooth mixture, before adding everything to the saucepan.)

Warm the pan over a medium heat for 5 minutes so it gently simmers, whisking every now and then. When warmed through and the spices are fragrant, pour straight into a mug.

To garnish, you could add a sprinkle of moringa powder and cinnamon and a couple of drops of coconut oil, if you like.

Drink it warm at night-time, right before bed.

Omi tí èyan ma mu koní sán kojá e̩

The water a person is destined to drink
always flows to them

Zobo

Serves 6 | 45 minutes, plus cooling time

Zobo is a hibiscus punch full of sensory contradictions, thanks to its mouthwatering tangy-sweet dryness. Bursting with more antioxidants than green tea, its taste is similar to cranberry juice, but even more refreshing. It's the ideal antidote to midday heat, and a superb way to harness this plant's full life-enhancing power.

60g/2¼oz dried hibiscus (zobo) leaves

7½cm/3in fresh ginger, sliced

skin (rind) of 1 pineapple (optional)

2 sticks of cinnamon

1 tbsp green cardamom pods

1 tsp nutmeg, grated

1 tbsp whole cloves

1 tsp whole black peppercorns

1 tbsp agave syrup (to taste)

2 tbsp lemon juice

3 tbsp caster sugar

1 pineapple wedge per glass (about 1cm/½in thick)

1 lemon slice per glass

Wash the hibiscus leaves, then drain and set aside. Boil 1 litre/1¾ pints water in a medium saucepan over a high heat. Stir in the hibiscus leaves along with the ginger, pineapple skin, all the spices and the pepper, then reduce to a simmer for 10 minutes.

Remove from the heat and allow the zobo to brew for 20–30 minutes. Strain the drink using a fine strainer or muslin cloth to remove all solids. Add the agave syrup to taste, stirring until completely dissolved. Dilute with water if you want a lighter flavour. Allow to cool, then store in the fridge until chilled.

To garnish your glass, pour the lemon juice into a shallow bowl, and shake the sugar onto a plate. Dip the rim of your empty glass into the lemon juice, and then into the sugar, picking up a nice generous amount. Push a pineapple wedge and a slice of lemon onto the sugared rim. Serve chilled, over ice.

Citrus Cocktail Ice Glass

Makes 1 | 20 minutes, plus freezing time

They're probably not advisable for your best dinner table – but I love making these ice glasses by freezing citrus-infused water. At pool parties, barbecues and cocktail parties, they come into their own and add a special touch to the occasion. Each glass lasts only for a drink or two (if you're fast!), so make as many as you need beforehand. And don't stop there; you can adapt it to make shot glasses and eccentric ice cubes, or add edible flowers, cucumber, fresh berries and herbs for an even more extravagant show.

1 medium plastic (or thick glass) cup

1 slightly smaller plastic (or thick glass) cup

1 sheet of aluminium foil

2 thin lemon slices

2 thin lime slices

2 thin orange or grapefruit slices

3 or 4 fresh mint leaves

Fill the medium-sized cup with water and place it in the sink. Put the smaller cup exactly in the middle of the medium one, letting any excess water spill out.

Put the lemon, lime and orange or grapefruit slices, halved or quartered as needed, and the mint leaves (or whatever ingredients you're using) into the water between the cups, spacing them all the way around.

Tightly wrap the cups with the foil to hold them in place, then pop them into the freezer. Leave for 3 hours, or until completely frozen. Take out of the freezer and remove the foil. Carefully remove the smaller cup; you may need to fill it briefly with warm water to loosen it.

Sometimes you'll find the bottom of the ice glass is thin and weak. To fix this, pour a little water into it and place it in the freezer again. When it's frozen, you can remove the outer cup, running it briefly under warm water to loosen it if you need to. Store the ice glasses in the freezer.

Index

UK/US Glossary

aubergine – eggplant
baking powder – baking soda
baking tray – baking sheet
beetroot – beet
caster sugar – superfine sugar
chicory – endive
clingfilm – plastic wrap
coriander – cilantro
cornflour – corn starch
courgette – zucchini
crisps – chips
frying pan – skillet
grill – broil/broiler
icing sugar – confectioners' sugar
plain flour – all-purpose flour
rocket – arugula
spring onions – scallions
starter – appetizer

Acknowledgements

I owe a particular debt to my youngest sister Alyx, for letting me keep our fridge and cupboards brimming with ingredients she wasn't allowed to touch, store stacks of various colourful backgrounds around our living room, and balance lighting equipment about the kitchen. She did move out, but promised it was not due to me.

Thank you to my family and extended family, especially my aunts Keffi and Teju, who kept me updated with a stream of family photographs, recipes and tips and tricks. Thank you to my incredible friends, especially Milly, Iman, Mike, Wase, Fiona and Temi, who have overwhelmed me with support from the very start.

Thank you to the Hoxton Mini Press team, who let me write this nutty little book. To Dani and Martin for their keen visual eye, Florence and Faith for their way with words, Ann and Anna, whose efforts kept things moving, Becca for her help editing the images, and Harry for his funny notes and commentary in drafting. Huge thanks to Emily, for testing every recipe in the book, even the crazier ones.

Thanks to Nina Olsson for being there for advice, and endless encouragement – it means a great deal.

Thank you to my readers; if you have bought or read this, I'm so lucky to have you.

Finally, thank you to my dad, for the wonderful heritage you have gifted me with. Your memory is cherished, and I am forever grateful for you, and our amazing, unique childhood in Ibadan.